ألف ليلة و ليلة

لطلاب العربية المصرية
(مستوى متوسط)

One Thousand and One Nights

for Intermediate Egyptian Arabic Language Learners

© 2023 by Matthew Aldrich

The author's moral rights have been asserted. All rights reserved. No part of this document may be reproduced or transmitted in any form or by any means, electronic, mechanical, photocopying, recording, or otherwise, without prior written permission of the publisher.

ISBN: 978-1-949650-94-5

Conceptualized by Matthew Aldrich

Written by Ahmad Al-Masri

Edited by Hend Khaled and Matthew Aldrich

Illustrations by Duc-Minh Vu

Audio by Mohamed Shehata

website: www.lingualism.com

email: contact@lingualism.com

Table of Contents

II .... INTRODUCTION
V .... HOW TO USE THIS BOOK

1 .... الفَصْل الأوّل: المَلِك شَهْرْيَار و الوَزير و بِنْتُه شَهْرزاد
Chapter 1: King Shahryar, the Vizier,
and his Daughter Scheherazade

11 .... الفَصْل الثّاني: قِصّةُ التّاجِر و الجِنّي
Chapter 2: The Tale of the Merchant and the Genie

23 .... الفَصْل الثّالِت: الصّيّاد و السَّمكة الذَّهبية
Chapter 3: The Fisherman and the Golden Fish

33 .... الفَصْل الرّابِع: علاء الدّين و المِصْباح السِّحْري
Chapter 4: Aladdin and the Magic Lamp

43 .... الفَصْل الخامِس: علي بابا و الأرْبعين حرامي
Chapter 5: Ali Baba and the Forty Thieves

53 .... الفَصْل السّادِس: الفَلّاح الذّكي و الجِنّي المُشاغِب
Chapter 6: The Clever Farmer and the Mischievous Genie

63 .... الفَصْل السّابِع: حرامي إسْكنْدِرية و رئيس الشُّرطة
Chapter 7: The Thief of Alexandria and the Police Chief

74 .... الفَصْل الثّامِن: الطّائِر الأزْرق
Chapter 8: The Blue Bird

84 .... الفَصْل التّاسِع: البِنْت و السّاحِرة
Chapter 9: The Girl and the Sorceress

94 .... الفَصْل العاشِر: الأمير و التِّنين
Chapter 10: The Prince and the Dragon

Introduction

"One Thousand and One Nights for Intermediate Egyptian Arabic Language Learners" is a captivating anthology designed specifically for adult Arabic language learners at the intermediate (B1-B2) level. This unique collection features the cherished classic tales in a simplified, yet engaging format, making it an excellent resource for those venturing into the enchanting world of Arabic language and literature.

The book comes with an array of special features to ensure an immersive and effective learning experience:

- **Diacritics for Pronunciation:** We've included diacritical marks (tashkeel) in the Arabic text to assist you in correct pronunciation, and to clarify the meaning of the words, easing your reading experience.

- **Professional Audio Accompaniment:** The book is supplemented with high-quality, slow-paced audio readings by a professional voice artist who is a native Arabic speaker from Egypt. This allows you to listen and mimic the correct pronunciation, intonation, and rhythm of Egyptian Arabic.

- **Comprehension Questions and Answers:** Each chapter is followed by a set of comprehension questions, along with their answers. This interactive feature helps to reinforce your understanding of the story and the language constructs used within it.

- **English Translations:** To support your learning, we've provided English translations of the stories. These can be used as a reference to cross-check your understanding of the Arabic text.

All these features work together to provide a comprehensive and enriching learning experience, ensuring you make consistent progress in your Arabic language journey.

The tales in this book have been carefully curated and reimagined to match the language proficiency of intermediate-level learners. We have incorporated level-appropriate vocabulary throughout the stories, ensuring you are neither overwhelmed by complexity nor left unchallenged. To enhance memorization and recognition, we've deliberately woven repetitive patterns of phrases and language structures into the text, encouraging natural language acquisition and recall.

Each chapter is short, and perfectly crafted to be absorbed in a single sitting, allowing you to steadily build your comprehension skills and vocabulary without feeling rushed. The stories retain the intrigue and charm of the original tales, providing you with a sense of accomplishment and enjoyment as you navigate your way through each tale.

As you delve into the enriched narratives found in "One Thousand and One Nights for Intermediate Egyptian Arabic Language Learners," you might notice an escalation in language complexity. If at any point the text appears too formidable, we would highly recommend you to revisit "One Thousand and One Nights for Elementary Egyptian Arabic Language Learners." The elementary-level book is meticulously designed to provide you with a firm grounding in the most common vocabulary used in the stories and acquaints you with straightforward sentence structures. Spending adequate time with the elementary book can help you grasp the fundamentals of the language effectively. Once you have a solid foundation and feel comfortable with the elementary material, we encourage you to return to the intermediate version. By then, the expanded vocabulary and more advanced sentence structures will no longer seem as daunting but will instead present a rewarding and manageable challenge, fostering your seamless progression towards mastery in Egyptian Arabic.

How to Use This Book

"One Thousand and One Nights for Intermediate Egyptian Arabic Language Learners" has been designed to offer flexibility to adapt to your individual learning style. Here's how you can utilize the features of the book according to your needs:

1. **Choose Your Approach:** You have the freedom to approach the stories in multiple ways. You could begin by tackling the Arabic text first, immersing yourself in the structure of the language and the flow of the story. Alternatively, you could start by listening to the accompanying audio, to attune your ear to the sound and rhythm of Egyptian Arabic. This can be particularly helpful if you are a more auditory learner.

2. **Use English Translations:** If you're finding the Arabic text or audio challenging, you can refer to the English translations to aid your understanding. Over time, as your comprehension improves, you could challenge yourself by attempting to read or listen to the Arabic without relying on the translations.

3. **Engage with Questions:** You can choose to tackle the comprehension questions before or after reading the story. Attempting them beforehand can provide a

focus for your reading, while answering them after allows you to assess your understanding of the text. Remember, the answers provided in the book are examples and your own answers, while differently worded, may still be correct.

4. **Repetition and Practice:** This book has been designed to promote repetition and practice, key strategies for language learning. We encourage you to revisit chapters and listen to the audio multiple times to reinforce your understanding and memorization.

Remember, the most effective learning strategy is the one that works best for you. So don't be afraid to experiment with different approaches until you find what suits you best.

Visit **www.lingualism.com/audio**, where you can find the free accompanying audio to download or stream (at variable playback rates).

الفَصْل الأوّل
المَلِك شهْرَيار و الوَزير و بِنْتُه شهْرزاد

كان يا ما كان في قديم الزّمان، كان فيه ملِك إسْمُه شهْرَيار بيِحْكُم ممْلكة كِبيرة و غنية. الملِك شهْرَيار كان بيِعْتِمِد على وَزيرُه الأمين الذّكي في إدارةِ أُمور الممْلكة. الوَزير كان عنْدُه بِنْت جميلة و ذكية إسْمها شهْرزاد، و كانِت مشْهورة بِذكاءْها النّادر و معْرِفتْها الواسْعة في

القِصص و التّاريخ.

في يوْم مِن الأيّام، عرِف الملِك شهْرَيار إنّ مِراتُه خانتُه، فا غِضب جِدّاً و زِعِل. قرّر شهْرَيار إنُّه يِتْجوِّز كُلّ ليْلة عروسة جِديدة، و يِقْتِلها تاني يوْم الصُّبْح علشان متِبْقاش عنْدها فُرْصة تخونُه. سُلوك الملِك شهْرَيار ده كان بِيْخوِّف كُلّ سِتّات و أهالي الممْلكة.

حسِّت شهْرزاد إنّها لازِم تِتْدخّل علشان تِنْقِذ سِتّات الممْلكة و تِرجّع الأمل لِشعْبها. اِقْترحِت على أبوها الوَزير إنّها تِتْجوِّز الملِك شهْرَيار. و رغْم قلقُه و خوْفُه على بِنْتُه، وافِق الوَزير على طلبْها علشان كان واثِق في ذكاءْها و حِكْمِتْها. قبْل الفرح، عمِلِت شهْرزاد خِطّة علشان تِقْنع الملِك إنُّه يِبطّل قتْل السِّتّات.

في ليْلة الفرح، طلبِت شهْرزاد مِن أُخْتها دينازاد تيجي معاها لِقصْر الملِك. دينازاد كانِت عارْفة خِطّةّ شهْرزاد و عارْفة إنّ دوْرْها هُوَّ المُساعْدة و الدّعْم. قبْل النّوْم، طلبِت شهْرزاد مِن دينازاد تُطْلُب مِنْها

تِحْكي قِصّة. بدأَت شهْرزاد تِحْكي قِصّة جميلة و شيِّقة للْملِك شهْرَيار. و وِقْفِت عنْد النُّصّ قبْل ما الملِك يِنامْ. كان دوْر دينازاد الأساسي هُوَّ إنّها تِفكّر شهْرزاد تِبْدأ القِصّة و تِبيِّنّ اِهْتِمامْها بيها، و ده خلّى الملِك يِحِسّ بِفُضول و يِحِبّ يِسْمع القِصّة هُوَّ كمان.

تاني يوْم الصُّبْح، كان الملِك شهْرَيار مُتشوِّق إنُّه يِسْمع باقي القِصّة. قرّر إنُّه مَيْموِّتْش شهْرزاد و إنُّه بِدّيها فُرْصة تِكمِّل القِصّة في اللّيْلة اللي بعْدها. بسّ شهْرزاد عِرْفِت إنّها لازِم تِكون ذكِية و تِخلّي كُلّ قِصّة تِطول أكْتر مِن ليْلة واحِدة عشان تِضْمن حَياتْها.

في اللّيْلة التّانْيَة، كمِّلت شهْرزاد القِصّة اللي بدإتْها، و اِبْتدِت قِصّة جديدة كمان. و في اللّيالي اللي بعْدها، فِضْلِت شهْرزاد تِحْكي القِصص الشّيِّقة و المثيرة اللي فيها دُروس و عِبر، و ده خلّى الملِك شهْرَيار يِنْبِهر بِذكاءْها و ثقافتْها.

كُلّ ليْلةْ، كانِت دنيازاد بِتِلْعب دوْر مُهِمّ في تحْميس الأجْواء و بِدايةْ القِصص. كانِت بتِفْضل صاحْيَة و بتِسْمع شهْرزاد باهْتِمام، و ده كان

بِيْزوّد فُضول الملِك و بِيحْفِزُه يِسْمع كُلّ كِلْمة بِتِتْقال.

في اللّيْلة الأولى مِن رِحْلِتْها الطَّويلة في القِصص و الحِكايات، بدأِت شهْرزاد تِحْكي قِصّة لِلْملِك شهْرَيار، قِصّة مليانة بالإثارة و المُغامْرة و الحِكْمة. و بِكِده اِبْتدِت رِحْلةْ شهْرزاد الشّجاعة و الحكيمة عشان تِنْقِذ سِتّات المملْكة و تِرجّع الأمن و السّلام لِشعْبها.

Questions

1. أيْه المُشْكِلة اللي كانِت عنْد الملِك شهْرَيار و أثّرِت على سِتّات الممْلكة؟

2. أيْه هِيَّ خِطّةْ شهْرزاد عشان تِنْقِذ سِتّات الممْلكة؟

3. إزّاي ساعْدِت أُخْت شهْرزاد، دنيازاد، في تنْفيذ الخِطّة؟

4. أيْه اللي الملِك شهْرَيار قرّر يعْمِلهُ بعْد ما سِمِع أوِّل قِصّة لِشهْرزاد؟

5. أيْه الهدف مِن إنّ كُلّ قِصّة تِطوّل لِأكْتر مِن ليْلة واحْدة؟

Answers

1. مُشْكِلِةْ الملِك شهْرَيار كانِت زعلُه بِسبب خِيانِةْ مِراتُه لُه، و قرارُه يِتْجوِّز واحْدة جِديدة كُلّ ليْلة و يِموِّتْها تاني يوْم الصُّبْح.

2. خِطِّةْ شهْرزاد هِيَّ إنّها تِتْجوِّز المِلك شهْرَيار و تِحْكيلُه قِصص مُشوِّقة كُلّ ليْلة عشان يِبطّل قتْل السِّتّات.

3. دنيازاد ساعْدِت شهْرزاد مِن خِلال إنّها تِفكّرْها إنّها تِبْدأ القِصّة و تِبيّن اِهْتِمامْها بيها، و ده خلّى المِلِك يِحِسّ بِفُضول و يِحِبّ يِسْمع القِصّة هُوَّ كمان.

4. قرّر المِلِك شهْرَيار إنُّه مَيموِّتْش شهْرزاد و إنُّه يِدّيها فُرْصة تِكمِّل القِصّة في اللِّيْلة اللي بعْدها.

5. الهدف مِن إنّ كُلّ قِصّة تِطوِّل لِأكْتر مِن ليْلة واحْدة هُوَّ إنّ شهْرزاد تِضْمن حَياتْها و يِكون عنْدها وَقْت كافي عشان تِقْنِع المِلِك يِبطّل يِقْتِل السِّتّات.

Chapter 1: King Shahryar, the Vizier, and his Daughter Scheherazade

In ancient times, a king called Shahryar ruled a vast and rich kingdom. King Shahryar relied on his trustworthy and intelligent vizier to manage the affairs of the kingdom. The vizier had a beautiful and clever daughter named Scheherazade, who was renowned for her exceptional intelligence and wide knowledge of stories and history.

One day, King Shahryar learned of his wife's infidelity, which filled him with great anger and sorrow. He decided to marry a new woman every night and kill her in the morning so that she wouldn't have the chance to betray him. This behavior of King Shahryar caused terror and panic among the women and people of the kingdom.

Scheherazade realized that she must intervene to save the women of the kingdom and restore hope to her people. She proposed to her father, the vizier, that she marry King Shahryar. Despite his concern and fear for his daughter, the vizier agreed to her request due to his trust in her intelligence and wisdom. Before the wedding, Scheherazade devised a plan to convince the king to stop killing the women.

On her wedding night, Scheherazade asked her sister, Dinarzad, to come with her to the palace of the king. Dinarzad knew of Scheherazade's plan and understood that her role was to assist and support her. Before sleep,

Scheherazade asked Dinarzad to request a story from her. Scheherazade began telling a fascinating and interesting story to King Shahryar and stopped in the middle before the king fell asleep. Dinarzad's main role was to remind Scheherazade to start the story and show interest in listening, which made the king curious and eager to hear the story as well.

The next morning, King Shahryar longed to hear the rest of the story. He decided not to kill Scheherazade and gave her a chance to finish the story the next night. But Scheherazade knew that she must be wise and make each story last more than one night to ensure her life.

On the second night, Scheherazade finished the story she began and started a new one. Over the following nights, Scheherazade continued telling thrilling and captivating stories that contained wisdom and morals, which astonished King Shahryar with her intelligence and culture.

Every night, Dinarzad played a vital role in enlivening the atmosphere and starting the stories. She remained awake and listened attentively to Scheherazade, which aroused the king's curiosity and motivated him to listen to every word uttered.

On the first night of this long journey of tales and stories, Scheherazade began telling a story to King Shahryar, a story full of excitement, adventure, and wisdom. And so began the brave and wise journey of Scheherazade to save the women of the kingdom and restore safety and peace to her people.

Questions

1. What was King Shahryar's problem that affected the women of the kingdom?
2. What was Scheherazade's plan to save the women of the kingdom?
3. How did Scheherazade's sister, Dinarzad, help execute the plan?
4. What did King Shahryar decide after hearing Scheherazade's first story?
5. What was the goal of making each story last more than one night?

Answers

1. King Shahryar's problem was his anger over his wife's infidelity and his decision to marry a new woman every night and kill her in the morning.
2. Scheherazade's plan was to marry King Shahryar and tell him thrilling and captivating stories every night to make him stop killing women.
3. Dinarzad helped Scheherazade by reminding her to start the story and show interest in listening, which made the king curious and eager to hear the story as well.

4. King Shahryar decided not to kill Scheherazade and gave her a chance to finish the story the next night.

5. The goal of making each story last more than one night was to ensure Scheherazade's life and give her enough time to convince the king to stop killing women.

الفصْل الثّاني
قِصّةُ التّاجِر و الجِنّي

في اللّيْلة التّانْية مِن قِصص شهْرزاد، اِبْتدِت بِقِصّة عن تاجِر غني و جِنّي قَوي جِدّاً. في يوْم مِن الأيّام، قرّر التّاجِر إنّهُ يِسافِر لِمدينة بِعيدة عشان يِبيع بِضاعْتهُ. قبْل ما يِبْتِدي رِحْلتهُ، وقِف في غابة هادْيَة عشان يِسْتريّح شُويّة و ياكُل.

في الغابة، قطع التّاجِر غُصْن شجرة عشان يِوَلَّع نار يِسخَّن بيها أكْلُه. بسّ فِجْأَة، ظهر جِنّي قَوي و غَضْبان جِدّاً قُدّام التّاجِر و صرخ و قالُه: "يا راجِل إنْتَ، إنْتَ قطعْت غُصْن الشجرة اللي أنا كُنْت ساكِن فيها، عشان كِده هقْتِلك!"

اِتْخضّ التّاجِر و اتْرعب، و اِبْتدى يِتْحايِل على الجِنّي علشان يِسامْحُه و يِسيبُه يعيش. قال لِلْجِنّي إنّ عنْدُه عِيْلة و صُحاب مُعْتمِدين عليْه و إنُّهم هَيموتوا مِن الزّعل لَوْ مات. سِمِع الجِنّي التّاجِر و قرّر إنُّه يِدّيلُه فُرْصة علشان يِكفّر عن غلْطِتُه.

وَعد الجِنّي التّاجِر إنُّه هَيسْمح لُه يِرجع لِعيلْتُه لِمُدِّة سنة واحْدة عشان يِوَدَّعْهُم و يِسدِّد دُيونُه، بسّ بِشرْط إنُّه يِرْجع بعْد ما تِعدّي السّنة دي عشان يِقْتِلُه. وافِق التّاجِر على الشّرْط و رِجِع لِمدينْتُه و قلْبُه ملْيان بِالزّعل و الخوْف.

و لمّا خِلْصِت السّنة، بدأ التّاجِر رِحْلِة الرّجوع لِلْغابة عشان يِواجُه مصيرُه اللي كان مكْتوب عليْه. و في الطّريق، قابِل راجِل عجوز ماسِك

عصايَة طَويلة. بدأ التّاجِر يِحْكيلُه قصِّتُه مع الجِنّي و عن الوَعد اللي وَعده بيه. صِعِب التّاجِر على العجوز و قرّر إنُّه يِمْشي معاه لِلْغابة.

و هُمّا في رِحْلِتْهُم، قابِل التّاجِر و العجوز اِتْنيْن رِجّالة تانْيين: واحِد شايِل جرَّةْ مايَّة و التّاني معاه حبْل طَويل. اِنْضمّ الاِتْنيْن دوْل لِلتّاجِر و الرّاجِل العجوز و راحوا كُلُّهُم لِلْغابة عشان يِواجْهوا الجِنّي.

لمّا وِصْلوا لِلْغابة، ظهر الجِنّي و هدِّد إنُّه يِقْتِل التّاجِر. اِتْدخِّل الرّاجِل العجوز و سأل الجِنّي لَوْ يِسْمحْلُه يِسْألُه تلات أسْئِلة قبْل ما يِقْتِل التّاجِر. وافِق الجِنّي على طلب الرّاجِل العجوز.

سأل العجوز السُّؤال الأوِّل عن نفْسُه: "ليْه العصايَة الطَّويلة دي مُفيدة لِيّا؟" و إجابْتُه كانِت إنُّه كان بِيِسْتخْدِمْها عشان يِقيس عُمْق النّهر قبْل ما يِعدّيه عشان يِضْمن سلامْتُه. و بعْديْن سأل العجوز السُّؤال التّاني: "أيْه فايْدِةْ الجرَّة؟" فا ردّ الرّاجِل اللي كان شايِل الجرّة إنُّه

بِيِسْتخْدِمْها عشان يِشيل فيها المايّة و يِقْدر يِطْفي بيها النّار لَوْ حصلِت حريقة. أخيراً، سأل العجوز السُّؤال التّالِت: "ليْه شايِل معاك الحبل الطَّويل ده؟" فا ردّ الرّاجِل التّالِت إنُّه بِيِسْتخْدِم الحبْل عشان يِتْسلّق بيه الجِبال و يِقْدر يِنْقِذ حَياةْ النّاس اللي محجوزين فوْقْها.

و بِناءً على رُدود الأسْئِلة التّلاتة دوْل، قال العجوز لِلْجِنّي: "الرِّجّالة دوْل اِسْتخْدِموا الأدْوات دي عشان يِساعْدوا و يِنْقِذوا النّاس، و ده بِيِعلِّمْنا إنّ الحَياة قيِّمة و لازِم نِعْمِل اللي نِقْدر عليْه عشان نِعيش في سلام و تعاوُن. ده مِش بِيِعلِّمك حاجة يا جِنّي؟" اِتْأثَّر الجِنّي بِكلام العجوز و قرّر يِسيب التّاجِر يِعيش و يِعْفي عنُّه.

بعْد التّجْرِبة المُرْعِبة الصّعْبة دي، رِجِع التّاجِر لِمدينْتُه و شكر الرِّجّالة التّلاتة على مُساعْدِتْهُم و تضْحِيِّتْهُم. و رغْم الخوْف و التّوتُّر اللي كان حاسِس بيهُم، إلّا إنّ التّاجِر اِتْعلِّم قيمةْ التّعاوُن و الصّداقة و عِرِف إنّ الحَياة بِتْعلِّمْنا دُروس و عِبر كِتيرة.

في الوقْت ده، كان الملِك شهْرَيار بِيِسْمع قِصِّة شهْرزاد بِاهْتِمام

شِديد. بدأ يِتْعلّق بِشخْصيّات القِصّة و يِتْعاطِف مع مشاعِرْهُم و معاناتْهُم. و بِفضْل القِصّة دي، اِبْتدى الملِك يِشوف الحَياة بِنظْرة جِديدة و يِعْرف إنّ النّاس مُمْكِن يِتْغيّروا و إنّنا بِناخُد الحِكْمة و العِبر مِن التّجارُب المُخْتلِفة.

في اللّيْلة اللي بعْدها، خلّصِت شهْرزاد قِصّةْ التّاجِر و الجِنّي و اِبْتدِت تِحْكي قِصّة جِديدة. و على الحال ده، فِضلِت شهْرزاد تِقوّي الثِّقة بينْها و بين الملِك شهْرَيار، و علِّمِتْه دُروس قيِّمة عن الحُبّ و الإنْسانية و العدْل مِن خِلال القِصص الرّائِعة اللي مِلْيانة بالْحِكم.

و مع كُلّ قِصّة شهْرزاد بِتِحْكيها، كانِت دينازاد معاها و بِتْساعِدْها علشان تِخلّي الملِك مُهْتِمّ و مُتشوِّق إنّه بِسْمع كمان و كمان. و بِالطّريقة دي، كانِت شهْرزاد بِتِنْقِذ نفْسها هيَّ و كُلّ سِتّات المملكة يوْم بعْد يوْم، و كانِت بِتْساعِد الملِك شهْرَيار إنّه يِفْهم و يِتْغيّر بِجدّ.

Questions

1. ليْه الجِنّي ظهر لِلتّاجِر و هدِّد إنُّه يِقْتِلُه؟

2. أيْه الشّرْط اللي حطُّه الجِنّي لِلتّاجِر قبْل ما يِقْتِلُه؟

3. مين النّاس اللي قابِلْهُم التّاجِر و هُوَّ رايِح يِواجِهْ الجِنّي؟

4. إزّاي الرّاجِل العجوز قِدِر يِقْنع الجِنّي إنُّه مَيِقْتِلْش التّاجِر؟

5. أيْه العِبْرة اللي اِتْعلِّمْها التّاجِر مِن القِصّة دي؟

Answers

1. ظهر الجِنّي للتّاجِر و هدّد إنُّه يِقْتِلُه عشان التّاجِر قطع غُصْن الشّجرة اللي هُوَّ ساكِن فيها.

2. الشّرْط اللي حطُّه الجِنّي هُوَّ إنُّه يِسمح للتّاجِر يِرْجع لِعيلْتُه لِمُدَّةْ سنة عشان يِودَّعْهُم و يِسدِّد دْيونُه، بسّ لازِم يِرْجع بعْد ما تِعدّي السّنة عشان يِقْتِلُه.

3. قابِل التّاجِر راجِل عجوز ماسِك عصايَة طَويلة، و راجِل شايِل جرّة مايّة، و واحِد تاني معاه حبْل طَويل.

4. قِدِر الرّاجِل العجوز يِقْنع الجِنّي إنُّه مَيِقْتِلْش التّاجِر عن طريق إنُّه يوَرّيه قيمةْ الحَياة و إزّاي مُمْكِن نِسْتخْدِم أدَوات مُخْتلِفة عشان نِعيش في سلام و تعاوُن.

5. التّاجِر اِتْعلِّم مِن القِصّة دي قيمةْ التّعاوُن و الصّداقة و عِرِف إنّ الحَياة بِتْعلِّمْنا دُروس و عِبر كِتيرة.

Chapter 2: The Tale of the Merchant and the Genie

On the second night of Scheherazade's stories, she began narrating a tale about a wealthy merchant and a powerful genie. One day, the merchant decided to travel to a faraway city to sell his goods. Before starting his journey, he stopped at a peaceful forest to rest and have his meal.

In the forest, the merchant cut a branch of a tree to light a fire and warm his food. Suddenly, a furious and powerful genie appeared before the merchant and yelled, "Oh human, you have cut the branch of the tree that was my shelter, and for that, I will kill you!"

The merchant was frightened and panicked, and he began pleading with the genie to forgive him and spare his life. He told the genie that he had a family and friends who relied on him, and they would die of grief if they lost him. The genie listened to the merchant and decided to give him a chance to make amends for his mistake.

The genie promised the merchant that he would allow him to return to his family for a period of one year to say goodbye to them and pay off his debts, but on the condition that he would return after the year had passed for the genie to kill him. The merchant agreed to the condition and returned to his city with a heavy heart filled with sadness and fear.

At the end of the year, the merchant started his journey back to the forest to face his inevitable fate. On the way, he met an old man carrying a long stick. The merchant narrated his story to the old man about the genie and the promise he made. The old man showed sympathy to the merchant and decided to accompany him to the forest.

As they continued their journey, the merchant and the old man met two other men: one carrying a jug of water and the other holding a long rope. The two men joined the merchant and the old man, and they all headed toward the forest to confront the genie.

When they reached the forest, the genie appeared and threatened to kill the merchant. The old man intervened and asked the genie if he would allow him to ask three questions before he killed the merchant. The genie agreed to the old man's request.

The old man asked the first question about himself, "How did the long stick benefit me?" and he answered that he used it to measure the depth of the river before crossing it to ensure his safety. Then the old man asked the second question, "What is the benefit of the jug?" and the man carrying the jug replied that he used it to store water and could use it to extinguish a fire in case of an emergency. Finally, the old man asked the third question, "Why are you carrying the long rope?" and the third man replied that he used the rope to climb mountains and could use it to save people stranded on its peaks.

Based on the answers of the three questions, the old man told the genie, "The three of us used these tools for help and survival, and this teaches us that life is valuable, and we must use what is in our hands to live in peace and cooperation. Didn't you consider that, O genie?" The genie was moved by the old man's words and decided to spare the merchant and forgive him.

After this terrifying and difficult experience, the merchant returned to his city and thanked the three men for their help and sacrifice. Despite his fear and the tension he went through, the merchant learned the value of cooperation and friendship and that life carries many lessons and wisdom.

Meanwhile, King Shahryar listened passionately to the story of Scheherazade. He began to develop an attachment to the characters of the story and sympathize with their feelings and struggles. Thanks to this story, the king began to see life through new eyes and realized that people could change and that wisdom and lessons come from different experiences.

On the following night, Scheherazade finished telling the story of the merchant and the genie and began to narrate a new story. In this way, Scheherazade continued to establish trust between her and King Shahryar and taught him valuable lessons about love, humanity, and justice through wonderful stories full of wisdom.

With each story told by Scheherazade, Dinarzad was always by her side, playing her role in making the king interested and eager to hear more. Thus, Scheherazade saved herself and the women of the kingdom day by day while leading King Shahryar toward true understanding and change.

Questions

1. Why did the genie appear to the merchant and threaten to kill him?
2. What was the condition that the genie set for the merchant before killing him?
3. Who were the people that the merchant met on his journey to confront the genie?
4. How did the old man manage to convince the genie not to kill the merchant?
5. What lesson did the merchant learn from this experience?

Answers

1. The genie appeared to the merchant and threatened to kill him because the merchant cut a branch from the tree, which was the genie's shelter.
2. The condition that the genie set for the merchant before killing him was to allow him to return to his

family for one year to say goodbye to them and collect his debts, but he must return after the year to be killed.

3. The merchant met an old man carrying a long stick, a man carrying a jar of water, and another holding a long rope.

4. The old man managed to convince the genie not to kill the merchant by showing the value of life and how different tools can be used to live in peace and cooperation.

5. The merchant learned from this experience the value of cooperation and friendship and that life holds many lessons and wisdom.

الفَصْل التّالِت
الصَّيّاد و السَّمكة الذَّهبية

في مَمْلكة بِعيدة، كان فيه صيّاد فقير عايِش مَع مِراتُه في كوخ صُغيّر على البحْر. كان بيِصْطاد علشان يِصْرِف على أُسْرتُه الصُّغيّرة. في يوْم مِن الأيّام، رمى الصيّاد شبكْتُه في البحْر علشان يِصْطاد سمك يبيعُه في السّوق. بعْد ما اسْتنّى ساعات طَويلة، لمَّ الشّبكة و لِقي فيها سمكة ذهبية صُغيّرة مَحْبوسة بيْن الحِبال.

اِتْفاجِئ الصّيّاد بِالِاكْتِشاف ده. و بصّ لِلسَّمكة الذّهبية اللي كانت بِتِلْمع بِأَلْوان جميلة في نور الشّمْس. فجْأة، اِتْبدِت السَّمكة تِتْكلِّم بِصوْت واضِح، و طلبِت مِن الصّيّاد يِسيبها تِعيش و هيَّ هتْحقّقْلُه تلات أُمنِيّات.

فكّر الصّيّاد في العرْض المُغْري ده، و بعْد تردُّد، قرّر إنُّه يِوافِق على طلب السّمكة الذّهبية. و بعْد ما الصّيّاد فكّها، طلب أُمنِيّتُه الأولى: بيْت جِديد و مُريح لأُسْرتُه. فا ظهر بيْت فخْم جنْب الكوخ القديم على طول.

الصّيّاد و مِراتُه مبْقوش مِصدّقين قدّ أيْه حظُّهُم سعيد، و شكروا السّمكة الذّهبية و عاشوا حَياة مُرفّهة في بيتْهُم الجِديد. بعْد مُدّة، قرّر الصّيّاد يِروح تاني لِلْبحْر علشان يُطلُب أُمنِيّتُه التّانْيَة: إنُّه يِبْقى غني و يِتْمتّع بِثرْوَة كِبيرة. و في اللّحْظة اللي اتمنّى فيها كِده، اِتملِت خزْنْة بيتُه بِالدّهب و الجَواهِر.

بِالثّرْوَة الكِبيرة دي، بقى الصّيّاد و مِراتُه مِن أغْنى النّاس في المَمْلكة.

اِشْتروا هُدوم فخْمة و عمِلوا عزايِم عشا لِصحابْهُم و جيرانْهُم، و عاشوا حَياةْ الأغْنِيا. و معَ ذلِك، اِبْتدى الصَّيَّاد يِحِسّ بِالْفراغ، و إنُّه عايِز حاجات أكْتر مِن كِده، فا قرَّر يُطْلُب أُمْنِيَّتُه التَّالْتة مِن السَّمكة الذَّهبية.

راح الصَّيَّاد لِلشَّطّ و نادى السَّمكة الذَّهبية، اللي طِلْعِت مِن المايَّة و سِمْعِت طلبُه. قال الصَّيَّاد: "عايِز أبْقى ملِك على المَمْلكة دي و أحْكُمْها بِعَدْل و رحْمة." وافْقِت السَّمكة الذَّهبية على طلبُه و اِتْحقَّقِت أُمْنِيَّتُه على طول.

الصَّيَّاد بقى ملِك عظيم و عاش في قصْر رائع معَ مِراتُه و أمْراؤُه. حكم بِعَدْل و رحْمة و حاوِل يِحسِّن حَياةْ شعْبُه. لكِن معَ مُرور الوَقْت، اِبْتدى يِعاني مِن القلق و الضُّغوط اللي بِتيجي معَ الحُكْم، و حسّ بِالتَّعب و الغضب مِن التَّحدِّيات اليَوْمية.

و في ليْلة هادْيَة، فكَّر الملِك الصَّيَّاد في حَياتُه و اِفْتكر الأيَّام البسيطة لمَّا كان بِيِصْطاد سمك و عايِش بِسلام معَ مِراتُه. قلْبُه وَجعُه لمَّا افْتكر إنّ الأيَّام دي راحِت، و قرَّر إنُّه يُطْلُب مُساعْدِةْ السَّمكة الذَّهبية تاني.

راح الملِك للشّطّ و نادى على السّمكة الذّهبية، اللي طلعِت مِن المايّة. طلب مِنْها ترجّعُه لِحَياتُه البسيطة اللي كان فيها صيّاد فقير، و تاخُد معاها كُلّ الثّرَوات و المُلْك. اِبْتسمِت السّمكة الذّهبية و وافْقِت على طلبُه، فا رِجِع الصّيّاد و مِراتُه لِلْكوخ البسيط على الشّطّ و عاشوا حَياة هادْيَة و سعيدة مِلْيانة بِالْمحبّة و الرِّضا.

طول الوَقْت ده، كان الملِك شهْرَيار بيِسْمع قِصّةْ شهْرزاد بِدهْشة و اِهْتِمام. بدأ يِتْعلّق بِشخْصيّةْ الصّيّاد و يِتْعِجب مِن حِكْمةْ السّمكة الذّهبية. بعْد ما شهْرزاد خلّصِت قِصّتْها، قال الملِك شهْرَيار إنُّه عايز يِسْمع قِصص أكْتر و إنُّه مِش هَيِقْتِلْها تاني يوْم الصُّبْح.

Questions

1. أيْه اللي لقاه الصّيّاد في شبكْتُه لمّا لمّها مِن البحْر؟

2. أيْه اللي عرضِتُه السّمكة الذّهبية على الصّيّاد مُقابِل تحْريرْها؟

3. أيْه الأُمْنية التّانْيَة اللي طلبْها الصّيّاد مِن السّمكة الذّهبية؟

4. كان أيْه شُعور الملِك الصّيّاد بعْد ما بقى ملِك على المملْكة؟

5. أيْه الطّلب الأخير اللي طلبُه الملِك الصّيّاد مِن السّمكة الذّهبية؟

Answers

1. لِقي الصّيّاد سمكة ذهبية صُغيّرة محْبوسة بيْن الحِبال.

2. عرضِت السّمكة الذّهبية تحْقيق تلات أُمْنيّات للصّيّاد مُقابِل إنُّه يِسيبْها تِعيش.

3. طلب الصّيّاد إنُّه يِبْقى غني و يِتْمتّع بِثرْوَة كِبيرة.

4. اِبْتدى الملِك الصّيّاد يِعاني مِن القلق و الضُّغوط اللي بِتيجي معَ الحُكْم، و حسّ بِالتّعب و الغضْب مِن التّحْدِّيّات اليَوْمية.

5. طلب الملِك الصّيّاد إنُّه يِرْجع تاني لِحَياتُه البسيطة اللي كان فيها صيّاد فقير، و تاخُد السّمكة الذّهبية معاها كُلّ الثرَوات و المُلْك.

Chapter 3: The Fisherman and the Golden Fish

In a distant kingdom, there was a poor fisherman who lived with his wife in a small hut by the sea. He relied on fishing to support his small family. One day, the fisherman cast his net into the sea in search of fish to sell in the market. After hours of waiting, he pulled up his net and found a small golden fish trapped among the ropes.

The fisherman was surprised by this discovery and marveled at the golden fish that shimmered in bright colors under the sunlight. Suddenly, the fish began to speak in a clear voice and asked the fisherman to spare its life in exchange for granting him three wishes.

The fisherman thought about this tempting offer and, after some hesitation, decided to agree to the golden fish's request. And when he released it, the fisherman made his first wish: a new and comfortable home for his family. A luxurious house appeared next to the old hut immediately.

The fisherman and his wife could not believe their good luck and thanked the golden fish. They lived a luxurious life in their new home. After some time, the fisherman wanted to go to the sea again to make his second wish: to become rich and have immense wealth. And at the moment he wished for it, his house was filled with gold and jewels.

With this immense wealth, the fisherman and his wife became some of the richest people in the kingdom. They bought luxurious clothes and held dinner parties for their friends and neighbors, and lived the life of nobles. However, the fisherman began to feel empty and wanted more, so he decided to make his third wish to the golden fish.

The fisherman went to the beach and called out to the golden fish that emerged from the water and listened to his request. The fisherman said, "I want to become the king of this kingdom and rule it with justice and mercy." The golden fish agreed to his request, and his wish was immediately granted.

The fisherman became a great king and lived in a magnificent palace with his wife and princes. He ruled with justice and mercy and sought to improve the lives of his people. But over time, he began to suffer from the increasing pressure and anxiety that comes with ruling, and felt tired and angry from the daily challenges.

On a quiet night, the fisherman king reflected on his life and remembered the simple days when he used to fish and live in peace with his wife. His heart ached for those days, and he decided to seek the help of the golden fish once again.

The king went to the beach and called out to the golden fish that emerged from the water. He asked her to return him to his simple life as a poor fisherman and to take all of his wealth and possessions with it. The golden fish smiled and granted his request, so the fisherman and his wife returned to their simple hut on the beach and lived a quiet and happy life filled with love and contentment.

Meanwhile, King Shahryar listened to Scheherazade's story with amazement and interest. He began to relate to the fisherman's character and admired the wisdom of the golden fish. After Scheherazade finished her story, King Shahryar announced that he wanted to hear more stories and that he would not kill her the next morning.

Questions

1. What did the fisherman find in his net when he pulled it out of the sea?
2. What did the golden fish offer the fisherman in exchange for its release?
3. What was the second wish that the fisherman asked the golden fish to grant him?
4. How did the king fisherman feel after becoming the ruler of the kingdom?
5. What was the last request that king the fisherman made to the golden fish?

Answers

1. The fisherman found a small golden fish trapped in the ropes.

2. The golden fish offered to grant three wishes to the fisherman in exchange for sparing its life.

3. The fisherman asked to become rich and enjoy immense wealth.

4. The king fisherman felt anxious and overwhelmed with the pressures that come with ruling, tired and angry with the daily challenges.

5. King fisherman asked to return to his simple life as a poor fisherman and for the golden fish to take all the wealth and the kingdom.

الفَصْل الرّابِع
علاء الدّين و المِصْباح السِّحْري

في اللّيْلة اللي بعْدها، بدأتِ شهْرزاد تِحْكي للْملِك شهْرَيار قِصّة ملْيانة تفاصيل مُشوِّقة عن علاء الدّين و المِصْباح السِّحْري.

علاء الدّين كان شاب فقير عايِش معَ أُمُّه الأرْملة في حيّ مِن أحْياء المدينة. كان بيِشْتغل الصُّبْح و بيِتْمشّى في الأسْواق و الشَّوارِع، و

كانِت أُمُّه بِتِعْمِل شُغْل البيْت.

في يوْم مِن الأيّام، و علاء الدّين بِيتْمشّى في السّوق، قابِل راجِل غريب قالُه إنُّه عمُّه اللي كانِت أُمُّه بِتِحْكي عنُّه. الرّاجِل الغريب قالُه إنُّه جِه علشان يِزور عيلْتُه، و إنُّه عارِف مكان سِرّي فيه كنْز كِبير مِسْتخبّي. الكِنْز ده مُمْكِن يِبْقى مُفْتاح الغِنى و النّجاح لعلاء الدّين و أُمُّه. و رغْم شُكوك علاء الدين، إلّا إنُّه قرّر يِروح معَ الرّاجِل الغريب يِدوّر على الكِنْز.

الرّاجِل الغريب وَصّلُه لِمغارة ضلْمة و مِسْتخبّية في الصّحْرا. طلب مِن علاء الدّين يِدْخُل المغارة و يِجيب المِصْباح القديم اللي فيها، و قالُه إنّ المِصْباح ده فيه قُوّة سِحْرية مِش مُمْكِن يِتْخيِّلْها. دخل علاء الدّين المغارة و لِقي المِصْباح السِّحْري. بسّ بِمُجرّد ما مِسكُه، قفل الرّاجِل الغريب باب المغارة و ساب علاء الدّين محْبوس جُوّاها، و كان ناوي إنُّه يِسْرق المِصْباح مِنُّه بعْد كِده.

في مُحاوْلة علشان يُخْرُج مِن المغارة، بدأ علاء الدّين يِدوّر على طريق

الخُروج. لِقي المِصْباح القَديم و فكّر إنُّه مُمْكِن يِنوّر بيه المغارة الضلْمة و يِدوّر على المخْرج. مِسِك المِصْباح السِّحْري و فجْأة ظهر جِنّي كِبير. قالُه الجِنّي: "أنا جِنّي المِصْباح السِّحْري، و أنا هِنا عشان أحقّقْلك تلات أُمْنِيّات تُطْلُبْها." علاء الدّين مكانْش فاهِم أيْه اللي بِيحْصل، بسّ قرّر إنّه يِسْتغِلّ الفُرْصة عشان يطْلع مِن المغارة. طلب مِن الجِنّي يِوَدّيه لِبيْتُه في المدينة، و في ثانْيَة واحْدة لِقي علاء الدّين نفْسُه جنْب أُمُّه اللي كانِت قلْقانة عليْه و مكانِتْش عارْفة أيْه اللي جراله. علاء الدّين قال لأُمُّه عن الجِنّي و المِصْباح السِّحْري. بدأوا يِفْهموا قُوّة المِصْباح و إزّاي يِقْدروا يِسْتخْدموه عشان يِحسّنوا حَياتْهُم.

طلب علاء الدّين مِن الجِنّي يجيبْلُهُم ثرْوَة كِبيرة تخلّيهُم يِعيشوا في رفاهية. و بِسبب الثّرْوَة دي، اِتْغيّرِت حَياةْ علاء الدّين و أُمُّه خالِص. اِشْتروا قصْر جميل و بقى علاء الدّين شخْصيّة مُهِمّة في المدينة. مَعَ الوَقْت، حسّ علاء الدّين إنُّه عايِز يِتْجوّز الأميرة الجميلة، بِنْت السُّلْطان. اِسْتخْدِم المِصْباح السِّحْري عشان يِساعْدُه يِكْسِب قلْب الأميرة و يِتْجوّزْها.

في الوَقْت ده، رِجِع الرّاجِل الغريب عشان يِرجّع المِصْباح السِّحْري اللي كان فاكِر إنُّه اِتْسرق مِنُّه. كان عايِز يِسْرقُه مِن علاء الدّين و يِسْتخدِم قُوّتُه عشان يِتْحكَّم في المدينة و يِفْرِض سَيْطرْتُه على سُكّانْها. بسّ علاء الدّين و الأميرة اِتْعاوْنوا مع َبعْض عشان يِقاوْموا الخطر اللي كان بِيْهدِّد حَياتْهُم و مُسْتقْبل المدينة.

في المعْركة الأخيرة، قِدِر علاء الدّين و الأميرة يِرجّعوا المِصْباح السِّحْري مِن الرّاجِل الغريب و يِهْزِموهُ. اِحْتفظ علاء الدّين بِالمِصْباح، بسّ قرّر إنُّه مِش هَيِعْتِمِد عليْه في المُسْتقْبل إلّا في حالات الضّرورة القُصْوى. اِتْجوِّز علاء الدّين الأميرة و عاشوا في تبات و نبات.

لمّا خلّصِت شهْرزاد قِصّة علاء الدّين و المِصْباح السِّحْري، كان الملِك شهْرَيار مُنْبِهِر بِالقِصّة و مِتْشوِّق إنُّه يِسْمع القِصص تانْيَة مُلْهِمة و مُثيرة. فِهِم الملِك شهْرَيار إنّ كُلّ قِصّة فيها دُروس مُهِمّة عن الحَياة و الحِكْمة و العدْل.

Questions

1. إزّاي علاء الدّين قابِل الرّاجِل الغريب؟

2. أيْه اللي طلبُه الرّاجِل الغريب مِن علاء الدّين لمّا خدُه المغارة؟

3. إزّاي علاء الدّين قِدِر يِهْرب مِن المغارة؟

4. إزّاي علاء الدّين اِسْتخْدِم المِصْباح السِّحْري عشان يِحسِّن حَياتُه هُوَّ و أُمُّه؟

5. أيْه الخطر اللي علاء الدّين و الأميرة واجْهوه؟

Answers

1. علاء الدّين قابِل الرّاجِل الغريب و هُوَّ بِيِتْمشّى في السّوق.

2. طلب مِن علاء الدّين يِدْخُل المِغارة و يجيب المِصْباح القديم اللي هِناك.

3. قِدِر علاء الدّين يِهْرب مِن المِغارة بِمُساعْدِةْ الجِنّي اللي طِلع لمّا فرك المِصْباح السِّحْري.

4. طلب علاء الدّين مِن الجِنّي يِجيبْلُهُم ثرْوَة كِبيرة، و ده سمحْلُهُم يِشْتِروا قصْر جميل و يِغيّروا حَياتْهُم خالِص.

5. الراجِل الغريب رِجِع عشان ياخُد المِصْباح السِّحْري و يِسْتخْدِم قُوَّتُه عشان يِتْحكِّم في المدينة، بسّ علاء الدّين و الأميرة وِقْفوا في وِشُّه و هزموهُ في المعْركة الأخيرة.

Chapter 4: Aladdin and the Magic Lamp

On the following night, Scheherazade began to tell an intricate and captivating story about Aladdin and the Magic Lamp to King Shahryar.

Aladdin was a poor young man who lived with his widowed mother in one of the city's neighborhoods. He worked during the day, wandering through the markets and streets, while his mother did household chores.

One day, while Aladdin was strolling through the market, he met a strange man who claimed to be his long-lost uncle, whom Aladdin had only heard about from his mother. The stranger claimed that he had come to visit his family and that he knew of a secret place where a great treasure was hidden. This treasure could be the key to Aladdin's and his mother's wealth and success. Despite his suspicions, Aladdin decided to join the strange man on a quest to find the treasure.

The man led him to a dark and secret cave in the depths of the desert. He asked Aladdin to enter the cave and retrieve the old lamp that was there, indicating that this lamp possessed an unimaginable magical power. Aladdin sneaked into the cave and found the magic lamp. However, once he held it, the stranger closed the cave's entrance and left Aladdin trapped inside, planning to steal the lamp from him later.

In an attempt to get out of the cave, Aladdin started looking for a way out. He found the old lamp and thought it might be useful to light up the dark cave and to search for the exit. He began to rub the magic lamp, and suddenly a giant genie appeared. The genie told him, "I am the genie of the magic lamp, and I am here to grant three wishes that you asked for." Aladdin did not fully comprehend what was happening, but he decided to seize the opportunity to escape from the cave. He asked the genie to transport him to his home in the city, and in the blink of an eye, Aladdin found himself next to his mother, who had been worried about her son's fate. Aladdin told his mother what had happened and about the genie and the magic lamp. They both began to realize the lamp's power and how it could be used to improve their lives.

Aladdin asked the genie to bring them immense wealth that would allow them to live in luxury. Thanks to this wealth, Aladdin's and his mother's lives changed completely. They bought a beautiful palace, and Aladdin became an important figure in the city. As time passed, Aladdin realized that he wanted to marry the beautiful princess, the sultan's daughter. He used the magic lamp to help him win the princess's heart and allow him to marry her.

In the meantime, the strange man returned to reclaim the magic lamp that he felt was stolen from him. He planned to steal it from Aladdin and use its power to control the city and impose his dominance over its inhabitants. But Aladdin and the princess cooperated to confront the danger threatening their lives and the future of the city.

In the final battle, Aladdin and the princess managed to retrieve the magic lamp from the strange man and defeat him. Aladdin kept the lamp but pledged not to rely on it in the future except in cases of extreme necessity. Aladdin and the princess got married and lived happily ever after.

Scheherazade finished telling the story of Aladdin and the magic lamp to King Shahriyar. The king was fascinated by this story and eager to hear more inspiring and exciting tales. King Shahriyar realized that every story carries important lessons about life, wisdom, and justice.

Questions

1. How did Aladdin meet the mysterious man?
2. What did the mysterious man ask Aladdin to do when he took him to the cave?
3. How did Aladdin escape from the cave?
4. How did Aladdin use the magic lamp to improve his and his mother's life?
5. What danger did Aladdin and the princess face?

Answers

1. Aladdin met the mysterious man when he was wandering in the market.

2. The mysterious man asked Aladdin to enter the cave and bring the old lamp that was there.

3. Aladdin managed to escape from the cave by requesting help from the genie who came out when he rubbed the magic lamp.

4. Aladdin asked the genie to bring them immense wealth, which allowed them to buy a beautiful palace and completely change their lives.

5. The mysterious man returned to retrieve the magic lamp and use its power to control the city, but Aladdin and the princess confronted him and defeated him in the final battle.

الفصل الخامِس
علي بابا و الأَرْبعين حرامي

لمّا خلّصِت شهْرزاد قِصّةْ علاء الدّين و المِصْباح السِّحْري، كان الملِك شهْرَيار مِسْتنّي بِفارِغ الصّبْر يِسْمع قِصص تانْية عجيبة و مليانة مُغامرات. و في اللّيْلة دي، بدأِت شهْرزاد تِحْكيلهُ قِصّةْ علي بابا و الأَرْبعين حرامي.

علي بابا كان راجِل بسيط و فقير، كان ساكِن في قرْيَة بِعيدة معَ مِراتُه و إبْنُه. و في يوْمٍ مِن الأيّامِ، كان علي بابا بِيْجمّع الحطب في الغابة لمّا سِمِع صوْت حَوافِر على الأرْض و رِجّالة بِيِتْكلّموا بِصوْت عالي. فجأةً ظهر قُدّامُه راجِل شكْلُه زعيم عِصابة مكوَّنة مِن أرْبعين حرامي، و لمّا وِصْلوا عنْد صخْرة كِبيرة، قال الزّعيم كِلْمةْ سِرّ: "اِفْتح يا سِمْسِم!" و فِعْلاً اِتْفتحِت الصّخْرة و ظهر مدْخل سِرّي لِمغارة كبيرة ملْيانة كُنوز و دهب.

بعْد ما الحراميّة مِشْيوا مِن المغارة، مِشي علي بابا لِلصّخْرة العِمْلاقة و اِسْتخْدِم كِلْمةْ السِّرّ عشان يِفْتح المدْخل. و لمّا دخل المغارة، اِتْفاجأ بِكمِّيّةْ الكُنوزالكِبيرة اللي عنْد الأرْبعين حرامي. قرّر علي بابا ياخُد شُويَّةْ دهب و يِرْجع بيه لِبيْتُه.

بعْد ما علي بابا رِجِع لِلْبيْت، حكى لِمْراتُه اللي حصل و قالّها عن الكنْز اللي لقاه. خبّوا الدّهب و اِتّفقوا يِسْتخْدِموه بِحِرْص عشان يِحسّنوا حَياتْهُم. بسّ علي بابا كان عنْدُه أخّ طمّاع إسْمُه قاسِمْ، و لمّا عِرِف اللي

حصل، كان عاوِز ياخُد جُزْء مِن الكِنْز لِنفْسُه.

راح قاسِم لِلْمغارة و اِسْتخْدِم كِلْمِةْ السِّرّ عشان يِفْتح المدْخل. لمّا دخل المغارة، مقْدِرْش يِتْحكِّم في طمعُه، و أخد كمّية كِبيرة مِن الدّهب و الكُنوز. بسّ لمّا حاوِل يُخْرُج، نِسي كِلْمِةْ السِّرّ و اِتْحبّس جُوّه الكهْف.

و قاسِم محْبوس جُوّه الكهْف، رِجِع الأرْبعين حرامي و لقوه. عاقْبوه و قتلوه عشان حاوِل يِسْرق كِنْزُهُمْ. لمّا عِرِفْ علي بابا اللي حصل لِأخوه، زِعِل و خاف. قرّر ياخُد اِحْتِياطات عشان يِحْمي عيلْتُه مِن الأرْبعين حرامي اللي هَيْحاوْلوا يِنْتِقْموا بِدون شكّ.

في نفْس الوَقْت، كان عِنْد علي بابا خدّامة ذكِية و مُخْلِصة إسْمها مُرْجانة. لمّا عِرْفِت خطر الحرامية، عمِلِت خِطّة عشان تِتْصرّف معاهُم. و بِمُساعْدِةْ علي بابا و إِبْنُه، قِدْرِت مُرْجانة تِقْضي على الأرْبعين حرامي و تِتْخلّص مِنْهُمْ بِشكْل نهائي.

بعْد ما قضوا على الأرْبعين حرامي، اِسْتمرّ علي بابا و عيلْتُه يِسْتخْدِموا

الكُنوز بِحِكْمة عشان يِحسّنوا حَياتْهُم و يِساعْدوا الفُقرا و المِحْتاجين في قَرْيِتْهُم.

اِتْجوّز إبْن علي بابا مُرْجانة كنوْع مِن التّقْدير لِشُجاعِتْها و ذكاءْها، و عاشوا كُلُّهُم حَياة سعيدة و مُسْتقرّة.

خلّصِت شهْرزاد قِصّةْ علي بابا و الأرْبعين حرامي، و كان الملِك شهْرَيار مُتحمّس إنُّه يِسْمع قِصّة جِديدة و مُلْهِمة في اللّيْلة اللي بعْدها.

Questions

1. عَلي بابا كان بِيِشْتغل أيْه؟

2. إزّاي علي بابا اِكْتشف مكان كِنْز الأرْبعين حرامي؟

3. قاسِم عمل أيْه لمّا عِرِف مَوْضوع الكِنْز؟

4. قاسِم مات إزّاي؟

5. مين هِيَّ مُرْجانة و أيْه دوْرْها في القِصّة؟

Answers

1. علي بابا كان راجِل بسيط و فقير بِيْجمّع حطب في الغابة.

2. اِكْتشفهُ و هُوَّ بِيْجمّع حطب و سِمِع صوْت حَوافِر على الأرْض و رِجّالة بِيِتْكلِّموا بِصوْت عالي. و شافْهُم بِيِسْتخْدِموا كلِمةْ السِّرّ عشان يِفْتحوا المغارة.

3. راح قاسِم لِلْمغارة و اِسْتخْدِم كِلِمةْ السِّرّ علشان يِفْتح الباب، و أخد كمّية كِبيرة مِن الدّهب و الكُنوز.

4. مات قاسِم لمّا الأرْبعين حرامي رِجْعوا و لقوه جُوّه المغارة و قتلوه عشان حاوِل يِسْرق كِنْزُهُم.

5. مُرْجانة كانِت خدّامة علي بابا الذّكية المُخْلِصة، و لِعْبِت دوْر مُهِمّ في التّخلُّص مِن الأَرْبعين حرامي بمُساعْدةْ علي بابا و إبْنهُ.

Chapter 5: Ali Baba and the Forty Thieves

When Scheherazade finished the story of Aladdin and the Magic Lamp, King Shahryar was excited to hear more amazing stories full of adventures. That night, Scheherazade began to tell the story of Ali Baba and the Forty Thieves.

Ali Baba was a simple and poor man who lived in a remote village with his wife and son. One day, while he was gathering firewood in the forest, he heard the sound of hooves on the ground and the loud voices of men. He saw a man who appeared to be the leader of a group of forty thieves, and when they approached a huge rock, the leader said a secret word: "Open sesame!" and the rock opened to reveal a secret entrance to a huge cave filled with treasures and gold.

After the thieves left the cave, Ali Baba approached the huge rock and used the secret word to open the entrance. When he entered the cave, he was amazed by the enormous treasures that the forty thieves possessed. Ali Baba decided to take some gold and return home with it.

After his return home, Ali Baba explained to his wife what had happened and told her about the treasure he had discovered. They hid the gold and decided to use it cautiously to improve their lives. However, Ali Baba had a greedy brother named Qasim, and when he discovered what had happened, he wanted to take a portion of the treasure for himself.

Qasim went to the cave and used the secret word to open the entrance. When he entered the cave, he could not control his greed and collected a huge amount of gold and treasures. But when he tried to leave, he forgot the secret word and became trapped inside the cave.

While Qasim was trapped inside the cave, the forty thieves returned and found him. They punished him severely and killed him for attempting to steal their treasure. When Ali Baba learned of his brother's fate, he felt sadness and fear. He decided to take measures to protect his family from the forty thieves, who would undoubtedly seek revenge.

At the same time, Ali Baba had a smart and loyal servant named Morgiana. When she learned of the danger posed by the thieves, she devised a plan to get rid of them. With the help of Ali Baba and his son, Morgiana was able to eliminate the forty thieves and get rid of them for good.

After defeating the forty thieves, Ali Baba and his family continued to use the treasure wisely to improve their lives and help the poor and needy in their village. Ali Baba's son married Morgiana in honor of her bravery and intelligence, and they all lived a happy and stable life.

Scheherazade finished telling the story of Ali Baba and the Forty Thieves, and King Shahryar was eager to hear a new and inspiring story the following night.

Questions

1. What was Ali Baba's profession?
2. How did Ali Baba discover the location of the Forty Thieves' treasure?
3. What did Qasim do when he learned about the treasure?
4. How did Qasim die?
5. Who is Morgiana, and what was her role in the story?

Answers

1. Ali Baba was a simple and poor man who collected firewood in the forest.
2. Ali Baba discovered the location when he was collecting firewood and heard the sound of horses' hooves and the noise of men speaking loudly, and saw them using the secret word to open the entrance to the cave.
3. Kasim went to the cave and used the secret word to open the entrance, and collected a huge amount of gold and treasures.
4. Kasim died when the Forty Thieves returned and found him inside the cave, and killed him for attempting to steal their treasure.

5. Morgiana was Ali Baba's smart and loyal servant and played a crucial role in getting rid of the Forty Thieves with the help of Ali Baba and his son.

الفَصْل السّادِس
الفَلّاح الذَّكي و الجِنّي المُشاغِب

في اللَّيْلة اللي بعْدها، بدإت شهْرزاد تِحْكي حِكايَة جِديدة لِلْملِك شهْرَيار عن فلّاح ذكي و جِنّي مُشاغِب.

كان فيه فلّاح فقير إسْمُه يوسِف عايِش في قرْيَة صُغيِّرة. يوسِف كان بيِشْتغِل كِتير عشان يِكْسب أكْل عيْشُه و يِقْدر يأكِّل أُسْرتُه. في يوْم

شمْسُه جميلة، قرّر يوسِف يِروح الغيْط عشان يُقْطُف شوَيَّةْ فاكْهة و خُضار يِبيعْهُم في السّوق. و هُوَّ بِيحْفُر في الأرْض، خبط الفاس بِتاعُه في جرَّة غَريبة مدْفونة تحْتَ الأرْض.

فتح يوسِف الجرَّة و لاقى جوَّاها جِنّي قديم مُشاغِب. قال الجِنّي لِيوسِف: "أنا محْبوس في الجرَّة دي بقالي سِنين طَويلة. شُكْراً عشان خرَّجْتني! بسّ لازِم أحذَّرك، أنا جِنّي مُشاغِب و بحاوِل أضْحك عليْك. هديك تلات أُمْنيّات، بسّ لازِم تاخُد بالك و تِفكَّر كُوَيِّس قبْل ما تُطْلُب حاجة."

يوسِف كان راجِل حكيم و ذكي و قرَّر إنُّه يِسْتخْدِم أمْنيّاتُه بحذر. أوِّل حاجة طلبْها إنُّه يِكون غني علشان يِقْدر يِوَفَّر حَياة أحْسن لِعيْلْتُه. الجِنّي إدّالُه دهب و جَواهِر كِتير، و دوْل غيَّروا حَياةْ يوسِف و عيْلْتُه لِحَياة مُرفَّهة.

بعْد كِده، طلب يوسِف مِن الجِنّي يِوَفَّر في قرْيتُه مايَّة نضيفة كِتير

لِلشُّرْب و الرّيّ. حقّق الجنّي الأُمْنية دي و ظهر نبْع جديد في القرْيَة بِتُخْرُج مِنُّه مايَّة نضيفة و مُنْعِشة.

و في الآخِر، طلب يوسِف مِن الجنّي يدّيلُه حِكْمة و فِهْم أَعْمق علشان يِساعِد أهْل قرْيتُه و يِحْميهُم مِن الخطر. وافِق الجنّي و إدّى يوسِف الحِكْمة و الفِهْم اللي طلبْهُم.

بِفضْل حِكْمِتُه الجديدة، قِدِر يوسِف يِساعِد النّاس في القرْيَة و يِلاقي حُلول مُبْتكرة لِلْمشاكِل و التّحدّيات اللي كانِت بِتْواجِههُم. مَعَ مُرور الوقْت، بقى يوسِف شخْصية مُحْترمة و مِتْقدّرة في قرْيتِه.

لكِن الجنّي مكانْش مبْسوط علشان مقْدِرْش يِخْدع يوسِف بالأُمْنيّات التّلاتة. قرّر الجنّي إنُّه يِحاوِل يِخْدع يوسِف بِطُرُق تانْيَة. اِبْتدى الجنّي يِعْمِل مشاكِل و فَوْضى في القرْيَة، زيّ تدْمير المحاصيل و حرْق البُيوت و التّوْقيع بيْن الفلّاحين.

اِسْتعْمِل يوسِف حِكْمِتُه و فِهْمُه عشان يِصلّح الضّرر اللي الجنّي اِتْسبِّب فيه و يِهدّي الأوْضاع المُتَوَتِّرة بيْن الفلّاحين. و بمُرور الوقْت، اِبْتدى

الجِنِّي يِفْهم إنُّه مِش هَيِقْدر يِضْحك على يوسِف و إنُّه قِدِر يِتْغلَّب على مكْرُه بِذكاءُه و حِكْمتُه.

في النِّهايَة، قرَّر الجِنِّي يِسيب يوسِف و قرْيتُه في سلام و يِروح يِدوَّر على حدّ تاني يِقْدر يِضْحك عليْه. و على الرَّغْم مِن إنّ الجِنِّي مِشي، لكِن يوسِف بِحِكْمتُه فِضِل يِساعِد الفلَّاحين و يِحسِّن حَياتْهُم.

بعْد ما الملِك شهْرَيار سِمِع قِصَّةْ الفلَّاح الذَّكي و الجِنِّي المُشاغِب، بقى مُتحمِّس عشان يِسْمع قِصص تانْيَة جميلة و مُلْهِمة فيها دُروس قيِّمة. و كِده، اِسْتنَّى بِفارِغ الصَّبْر بِدايَةْ القِصَّة الجايَّة اللي شهْرزاد هتِحْكيها.

Questions

1. أيْه اللي لاقاه يوسِف لمّا فاسُه خبط في جرّة غريبة مدْفونة تحْتَ الأرْض؟

2. كام كان عدد الأُمْنيّات اللي الجِنّي إدّاها لِيوسِف؟ و أيْه هُما؟

3. إزّاي يوسِف اِسْتخْدِم الحِكْمة اللي الجِنّي إدّاهالهُ؟

4. الجِنّي عمل أيْه لمّا مقْدِرْش يِخْدع يوسِف بالأُمْنيّات التّلاتة؟

5. يوسِف عمل أيْه عشان يواجِهْ المشاكِل اللي سبّبها الجِنّي في القرْيَة؟

Answers

1. لِقي يوسِف جِنّي قديم مُشاغِب مَحْبوس جُوّا الجرّة.

2. الجني إدى يوسِف تلات أُمْنِيّات: إنُّه يِبْقى غني، و يِجيب مايّة نضيفة كِتير لِقَرْيتُه، و يِدّيلُه حِكْمة و فِهْم عميق.

3. اِسْتخْدِم يوسِف الحِكْمة عشان يِساعِد الفلّاحين في حلّ مشاكِلْهُم و يِلاقي حُلول مُبْتكِرة للتّحدّيّات اللي كانوا بِيْواجْهوها.

4. قرّر الجِنّي إنُّه يِحاوِل يِخْدع يوسِف بِطُرْق تانْيَة و بدأ يِعْمِل مشاكِل و فَوْضى في القَرْيَة.

5. اِسْتخْدِم يوسِف حِكْمتُه و فِهْمُه عشان يِصلّح الأضْرار اللي سبّبها الجِنّي و يِهدّي الوَضْع المُتَوَتِّر بينْ الفلّاحين.

Chapter 6: The Clever Farmer and the Mischievous Genie

On the following night, Scheherazade began telling another story to King Shahryar about a clever farmer and a mischievous genie.

There was a poor farmer named Youssef who lived in a small village. Youssef worked hard to provide for his family and make ends meet. One sunny day, he decided to go to the field to pick some fruits and vegetables to sell at the market. While plowing the land, his plow hit a strange jar buried in the ground.

Youssef opened the jar to find an old and mischievous genie inside. The genie said to Youssef, "I have been trapped in this jar for centuries. Thank you for freeing me! But I must warn you, I am a mischievous genie, and I will try to deceive you. I will grant you three wishes, but you must be careful and think carefully before you ask for anything."

Youssef was a wise and clever man and decided to use his wishes carefully. He first wished to be rich so that he could provide a better life for his family. The genie granted him a lot of gold and jewels that turned Youssef and his family's life into a luxurious one.

Then, Youssef asked the genie to provide his village with clean and abundant water for drinking and irrigation. The genie also granted this wish, and a new spring appeared in the village that flowed with clean and refreshing water.

Finally, Youssef asked the genie to grant him wisdom and deeper understanding to help his village people and protect them from danger. The genie agreed and gave Youssef the wisdom and understanding he asked for.

With his new wisdom, Youssef was able to help the villagers solve their problems and find innovative solutions to the challenges they faced. Over time, Youssef became a respected and appreciated figure in his village.

However, the genie was not happy that he could not deceive Youssef with his three wishes. He decided to try to deceive Youssef in other ways. The genie began causing problems and chaos in the village, such as destroying crops, setting fire to homes, and inciting fights among villagers.

Youssef used his wisdom and understanding to fix the damage caused by the genie and calm the tense situations among the villagers. Over time, the genie realized that he could not deceive Youssef and that he had been defeated by his intelligence and wisdom.

In the end, the genie decided to leave Youssef and his village in peace and go in search of another person he could deceive. Despite the genie's departure, Youssef's wisdom continued to help the villagers and improve their lives.

After hearing the story of the clever farmer and the mischievous genie, King Shahryar became eager to hear more wonderful and inspiring stories that carry valuable lessons. And so, he eagerly awaited the start of the next story that Scheherazade would tell.

Questions

1. What did Youssef find when his plow collided with a strange jar buried underground?
2. How many wishes did the genie grant Youssef, and what were those wishes?
3. How did Youssef use the wisdom that the genie gave him?
4. What did the genie do when he couldn't deceive Youssef with his three requests?
5. What did Youssef do to confront the problems caused by the genie in the village?

Answers

1. Youssef found an old and mischievous genie trapped inside the jar.
2. The genie granted Youssef three wishes: to become rich, to provide his village with pure and abundant

water, and to give him wisdom and deeper understanding.

3. Youssef used the wisdom to help the villagers solve their problems and find innovative solutions to the challenges they faced.

4. The genie decided to try to deceive Youssef in other ways and began to cause problems and chaos in the village.

5. Youssef used his wisdom and understanding to repair the damage caused by the genie and calm the tense situations among the villagers.

الفَصْل السّابِع
حرامي إسْكِنْدِرية و رئيس الشُّرطة

في اللّيْلة اللي بعْدها، بدإتْ شهْرزاد تِحْكي قِصّةْ حرامي إسْكِنْدِرية و رئيس الشُّرطة لِلْملِك شهْرَيار.

في مدينةْ إسْكِنْدِرية العريقة، كان فيه لِصّ شاطِر و مكّار إسْمهُ ياسِر، كان بيِسْرق فِلوس النّاس الأغْنيا و محدِّش بيِقْدر يُقْبْض عليْه. كان ياسِر

بِيْخطّط كُوَيِّس لِكُلّ عمليةْ سرْقة، كان بِيدْرِس البيوت و نشاط الضّحايا اليَوْمي قبْل ما يْنفِّذ خِطّتُه.

في يوْم مِن الأيّام، سرق ياسِر بيْت تاجِر غني. صِحي التّاجِر الصُّبح لِقي إنّ كُلّ مُمْتلِكاتُه الغالْيَة اِخْتِفِت و ملْهاش أثر. على طول راح لِرئيس الشُّرْطة، و ده كان راجِل حكيم و جادّ و إسْمُه عبْد الرّحمن، و قالّه على الحادْثة. قال التّاجِر: "سرقوا كُلّ ثرْوِتي! مفيش غيْر حرامي إسْكِنْدِرية المشْهور اللي عمل كِده."

حسّ رئيس الشُّرْطة عبْد الرّحْمن بِالْفُضول بِسبب مهارات الحرامي العجيبة، و قرّر يُوَقّف جرايِم السّرِقة دي و يُقْبِض على الحرامي بِنفْسُه. بدأ عبْد الرّحْمن يحقّق و يِجمّع معْلومات عن السّرْقات و يدوّر على تفاصيل تِساعْدُه يِوْصل لِلْحرامي.

في ليْلة مِن اللّيالي، اِكْتِشف عبْد الرّحْمن إنّ فيه حرامي ناوي يسْرق قصْر واحِد مِن الأغْنِيا. قرّر عبْد الرّحْمن إنّه يِترصّدْلُه. و في نُصّ اللّيل،

شاف عبْد الرّحْمن ياسِر بِيدْخُل القصْر و بِيسْتخْدِم حبْل عشان يِتْشعْبط على الحيْط.

لمّا دخل ياسِر القصْر، لِقِي عبْد الرّحْمن مِسْتنّيه. قال عبْد الرّحْمن بِصوْت هادي: "خلاص يا ياسِر، مُغامْراتك خِلْصِت، إنْتَ دِلْوَقْتي قُدّام رئيس الشُّرْطة."

اِتْفاجِئ ياسِر لمّا شاف عبْد الرّحْمن، بسّ مِسْتسْلِمْش بِسُهولة. قال ياسِر: "جايِز حظّك كان حِلْو المرّة دي، بسّ مِش هتِقْدر تُقْبُض على كُلّ الحرامية في إسْكِنْدِرية."

ردّ عبْد الرّحْمن بِثِقة: "جايِز، بسّ النّهارْده هقْدر أمْسِك أشْهر و أذْكى واحِد فيهُم."

قِدِر عبْد الرّحْمن يُقْبُض على ياسِر بعْد مطارْدة قُصيّرة جُوّا القصْر. ياسِر اِتْقبض عليْه، و اِتْحكم عليْه بِالإدانة في كُلّ جرايمْه. في المحْكمة، سأل القاضي ياسِر: "ليْه قرّرْت تِبْقى حرامي و تِسْرق مِن النّاس بدل ما تِكْسب رِزْقك بِطريقة شرْعية؟"

ردّ ياسِر: "كُنْت فقير و مكانْش عنْدي مهارات وَلا تعْليم يخلِّيني أعيش بِكرامة. أنا مكُنْتِش عايِز أضُرّ حدّ، بسّ الظُّروف خلّتْني أختار المصير دَه."

فِهِم عبْد الرّحْمن إنّ الظُّروف الصّعْبة كانِت سبب رئيسي وَرا اِخْتِيار ياسِر لِحَياةْ الجريمة. قرّر عبْد الرّحْمن يِساعِد ياسِر يغيِّر حَياتُه و يِدّيلُه فُرْصة علشان يِبْقى شخْص أحْسن. بعْد ما ياسِر خلّص مُدّةْ عُقوبتُه، جابْلُه عبْد الرّحْمن فُرْصة إنُّه يِشْتغل حارِس لِبيْت واحِد مِن التُّجار الأغْنِيا.

خلّصِت شهْرزاد قِصّةْ حرامي إسكِنْدرية و رئيس الشُّرْطة. القِصّة عجبِت الملِك شهْرَيار و كان عايِز يِسْمع قِصص تانْيَة مُلْهِمة و مُثيرة. بِالطّريقة دي، شهْرزاد خلّت الملِك شهْرَيار يِسْتنّى لِليْلة اللي بعْدها علشان يِسْمع قِصّة تانْيَة.

القِصّة دي علّمِت الملِك شهْرَيار و النّاس اللي سِمْعوها إنّ الظُّروف

الصّعْبة مُمْكِن تِجْبِر بعْض النّاس إنّهُم يِعْمِلوا تصرُّفات غلط، بسّ لِسّه فيه أمل إنّهُم يغيّروا حَياتْهُم و يِسْعوا لِمُسْتقْبل أحْسن بمُساعْدِة غيرْهُم. فِهِم الملِك إنّ العدْل و الرّحْمة لازِم يِكونوا مَوْجودين في حُكْمُه و إنُّه لازِم يِكون مُسْتعِدّ يِدّي فُرص تانْيَة للْمُسْتضْعفين في مملْكتُه.

Questions

1. أيْه هُوَّ إسْم الحرامي اللي كان بِيِسْرق فِلوس النّاس الأغْنِيا في إسْكِنْدِرية؟

2. ياسِر كان بيِعْمِل أيْه قبْل ما يِنفِّذ خِطط السِّرْقة؟

3. مين رئيس الشُّرْطة اللي قرّر يِوَقِّف جرايِم السِّرْقة بِتاعِةْ ياسِر؟

4. إزّاي عبْد الرّحْمن قِدِر يُقْبُض على ياسِر؟

5. ازاي عبْد الرّحْمن ساعِد ياسِر بعْد ما اِنْتهِت مُدِّةْ عُقوبْتُهْ؟

Answers

1. إسْم الحرامي هُوَّ ياسِر.

2. كان ياسِر بِيْخطّط كُوَيِّس لِكُلّ عمليةْ سِرْقة، عشان كِده كان بيِدْرِس البيوت و النّشاط اليَوْمي للضّحايا قبْل ما يِنفِّذ خِطّتُه.

3. عبْد الرّحْمن هُوَّ رئيس الشُّرْطة اللي قرّر يِعْمِل كِده.

4. عبْد الرّحْمن اِكْتشف إنَّ الحرامي ناوي يِسْرق قصْر واحِد مِن الأغْنِيا، و اِتْرصّدْلُه.

5. عبْد الرّحْمن وَفّرْلُه فُرْصة إنُّه يِشْتغِل حارِس لِبيْت واحِد مِن التُّجار الأغْنِيا.

Chapter 7: The Thief of Alexandria and the Police Chief

The next night, Scheherazade began to tell the story of the Alexandria Thief and the Chief of Police to King Shahryar.

In the ancient city of Alexandria, there was a skilled and cunning thief named Yaser who robbed the wealth of rich people without being caught. Yaser planned carefully for each theft, and he studied the houses and daily schedules of his victims before executing his plans.

One day, Yaser stole from the house of a wealthy merchant. The merchant woke up to find that all his valuable possessions had disappeared without a trace. Immediately, he went to the Chief of Police, a wise and strict man named Abdulrahman, to report the incident. The merchant said, "All my wealth has been stolen! This can only be the work of the notorious Thief of Alexandria."

The extraordinary abilities of the thief intrigued the Chief of Police, Abdulrahman, who decided to put an end to these thefts and capture the thief himself. Abdulrahman began investigating and gathering information about the thefts and searching for details that could help him reach the thief.

One night, Abdulrahman discovered that the thief was planning to steal the palace of a nobleman. Abdulrahman decided to wait for him in ambush. And at midnight,

Abdulrahman saw Yaser sneaking into the palace and using a rope to climb the wall.

When Yaser entered the palace, he found Abdulrahman waiting for him patiently. Abdulrahman said calmly, "Your adventures have come to an end, Yaser. You are now in the hands of the Chief of Police."

Yaser was surprised by the presence of Abdulrahman, but he did not surrender easily. He said, "Maybe you were lucky this time, but you won't be able to catch all the thieves in Alexandria."

Abdulrahman answered confidently, "It may be true, but today I will be able to catch the most famous and cunning of them."

Abdulrahman managed to catch Yaser after a short chase inside the palace. Yaser was arrested and convicted of all his crimes. In court, the judge asked Yaser, "Why did you decide to become a thief and steal from people instead of earning your living legally?"

Yaser answered, "I was poor and had no skills or education that could enable me to live with dignity. I didn't want to hurt anyone, but circumstances forced me to choose this fate."

Abdulrahman realized that harsh circumstances were the main reason behind Yaser's choice of a life of crime. He decided to help Yaser change his life and provide him with an opportunity to become a better person. After Yaser served his sentence, Abdulrahman provided him with a job opportunity as a guard in a a wealthy merchant's house.

Scheherazade finished telling the story of the Alexandria thief and the police chief. King Shahryar was impressed by this story and wanted to hear more inspiring and exciting stories. Thus, Scheherazade forced King Shahryar to wait until the next night to hear another story.

This story taught King Shahryar and the people who heard it that harsh circumstances could force some people to commit bad deeds, but there is still hope to redirect their lives and work towards a better future with the help of others. The king remembered that justice and mercy should prevail in his rule and that he should be prepared to provide second chances to the less fortunate in his kingdom.

Questions

1. What is the name of the thief who was stealing the wealth of rich people in Alexandria?
2. What was Yaser doing before carrying out his robbery plans?
3. Who is the police chief who decided to put an end to Yaser's robberies?
4. How did Abdulrahman manage to arrest Yaser?

5. How did Abdulrahman help Yaser after he served his sentence?

Answers

1. Yaser is the name of the thief.
2. Yaser was carefully planning each robbery, where he would study the houses and the daily schedules of his victims.
3. Abdulrahman is the police chief who made that decision.
4. Abdulrahman discovered that the thief planned to steal from the palace of a nobleman and waited for him in an ambush.
5. Abdulrahman provided him with a job opportunity as a guard in a a wealthy merchant's house.

الفصْل التّامِن
الطّائِر الأزْرق

في اللّيْلة اللي بعْدها، بدأت شهْرزاد تِحْكي لِلْمَلِك شهْرَيار قِصّةْ الطّائِر الأزْرق.

في بلد بِعيدة كان فيه ملِك طيِّب و مِراتُه الملِكة. كان عنْدُهُم بِنْت جميلة إسْمها الأميرة ليْلى. معَ إنّها كانِت جميلة و نبيلة، بسّ ليْلى كانِت

حزينة لإنّها ملقِتْش حُبّ حَياتْها. في يوْم مِن الأيّام و هيَّ بتِتْمشَّى في جِنيْنِةْ القصْر، سِمْعِت طائر بيْغنّي بِصوْت جميل و لوْنُه أزْرق زاهي، طائر محدِّش شاف زيُّه قبْل كِده.

فكّرِت الأميرة ليْلى إنّ الطّائر الأزْرق ده مُمْكِن يكون مُفْتاح سعادِتْها، فا قرّرِت إنّها تِدوّر عليْه. طلبِت مِن والدْها الملِك يِعْلِن مُسابْقة يُطْلُب فيها مِن المُشارِكين إنّهُم يِدوّروا على الطّائر الأزْرق و يجيبوهولْها. وافِق الملِك على الفِكْرة و أعْلن المُسابْقة لِكُلّ شباب المملْكة.

اِتْزاحِم الشباب على القصْر علشان يِتْنافْسوا في المُسابْقة و يِدوّروا على الطّائر الأزْرق. مِن بيْن النّاس المُشارِكين، كان فيه شابّ فقير إسْمُه ياسين. ياسين كان بيْحِبّ الأميرة ليْلى، و كان عايِز يفرّحْها بإنُّه يِلاقي الطّائر الأزْرق. مكانْش عنْدُه ثرْوة وَلا منْصِب يخلّوه مُناسِب للأميرة، بسّ كان ذكي و شُجاع و عنْدُه إصْرار.

بدأ ياسين رِحْلتُه الطّويلة علشان يِدوّر على الطّائر الأزْرق. مرِّت الأيّام و الأسابيع و الشُّهور مِن غيْر فايْدة. و في الرِّحْلة دي، قابِل ياسين ناس

كِتير ساعْدوهُ و قالولهُ معْلومات جِديدة عن مكان الطّائِر الأزْرق.

في النِّهاية، اِكْتشف ياسين إنّ الطّائِر الأزْرق عايِش في جِزيرة بِعيدة في وُسْط البحْر. قرّر ياسين يِروح لِلْجِزيرة دي علشان يجيب الطّائِر و يِرْجع بيه لِلْأميرة ليْلى. بعْد أيّام طَويلة مِن التّعب و العَواصِف الشّديدة في البحْر، وِصِل ياسين لِلْجِزيرة البِعيدة.

اِبْتدى ياسين يِسْتكْشِف الجِزيرة و قابِل عقبات و مخْلوقات غريبة، بسّ ماسْتسْلِمْش. بعْد بحْث صعْب و إصْرار، لِقي ياسين الطّائِر الأزْرق و قِدِر يِمْسِكُه. رِجِع ياسين، و هُوّ فرْحان جِدّاً، بِالطّائِر الأزْرق لِلْممْلكة.

لمّا رِجِع ياسين و ورّى الطّائِر الأزْرق لِلْأميرة ليْلى، فِرِح النّاس كُلُّهُم و اِنْدهشوا. اِحْتفل الملِك بِرُجوع ياسين و أعْلن إنُّه كسب المُسابْقة. بسّ الأميرة ليْلى مكانِتْش عايْزة بسّ الطّائِر الأزْرق، كمان كانِت عايْزة الشّابّ اللي راح لِآخِر الدُّنْيا علشان يِفرّحْها.

اِتْجوِّزِت الأميرة ليْلى ياسين، بعْد مُوافْقةْ الملِك و الملِكة. عاش ياسين

و الأميرة ليلى حياة سعيدة مليانة بالحبّ و الرّفاهية. و علِّمِت القصّة الملِك شهْرَيار و النّاس إنّ الإصرار و الشّجاعة و الحُبّ بيِقْدروا يِتْغَلّبوا على أيّ تحدّي و مُمْكِن يِوَصّلوا النّاس للسّعادة الحقيقية.

و بِكِده، خِلِص الفصْل التّامِن مِن حِكايات ألْف ليْلة و ليْلة. مكانْش قُدّام الملِك شهْرَيار غيْر إنّه يِسْتنّى بِفارِغ الصّبْر للّيْلة اللي جايّة علشان يِسْتمْتع بِقِصّة جديدة تِحْكيهاله شهْرزاد.

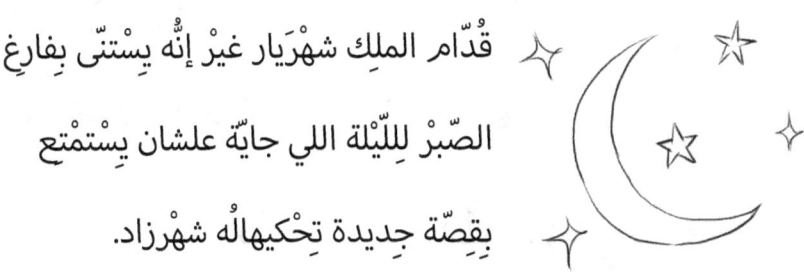

في اللّيْلة اللي بعْدها، اتْقابِل الملِك شهْرَيار و شهْرزاد تاني. و كان الملِك مُتحمِّس جداً إنُّه يِسْمع قِصص تانْية مُلْهِمة و مُثيرة. حسّ الملِك شهْرَيار إنّ الحِكايات دي غيّرِت حَياتُه للأحْسن، و إنّها علّمِتُه دُروس قيِّمة عن العدْل و الحِكْمة و الحُبّ.

و على الحال ده، فِضْلِت شهْرزاد تِحْكي قِصصْها لِلمَلِك شهْرَيار ليْلة وَرا ليْلة، في مُحاوْلة إنّها تعلّمُه و تِعلِّم شعْبُه دُروس تانْية مُهمّة عن الحَياة و الإنْسانية.

Questions

1. الأميرة ليْلى كانِت حاسّة بِأيْه؟ و ليْه؟

2. أيْه اللي الأميرة ليْلى طلبِتُه مِن والِدْها الملك؟

3. مين ياسين؟ و أيْه اللي خلّاه يِشْترِك في المُسابْقة؟

4. ياسين عِرِف إنّ الطائِر الأزْرق ساكِن فيْن؟

5. أيْه اللي حصل لمّا رِجِع ياسين بِالطّائِر الأزْرق لِلْممْلكة؟

Answers

1. كانِت الأميرة ليْلى حاسّة بِالْحُزْن عشان ملقِتْش حُبّ حَياتْها.

2. طلبِت الأميرة ليْلى مِن والِدْها الملِك إنُّه يِعْلِن مُسابْقة يُطْلُب فيها مِن المُشاركين إنُّهُم يِدوّروا على الطّائِر الأزْرق و يِجيبوهولْها.

3. ياسين هُوَّ شابّ فقير كان بِيْحِبّ الأميرة ليْلى و عايِز يِفرّحْها بِإنُّه يِجيبْلها الطّائِر الأزْرق.

4. عِرِف ياسين إنّ الطّائِر الأزْرق كان عايِش في جِزيرة بِعيدة في وُسْط البحْر.

5. اِتْملِت قُلوب النّاس بِالْفرْحة و الدّهْشة لمّا رِجِع ياسين بِالطّائِر الأزْرق، و اِحْتفل الملِك بِفوْزُه في المُسابْقة، و اِتْجوّزِت الأميرة ليْلى ياسين.

Chapter 8: The Blue Bird

On the following night, Scheherazade began to tell King Shahryar the story of the Blue Bird.

In a faraway land, there was a kind king and his queen. They had a beautiful daughter named Princess Leila. Despite her beauty and nobility, Leila felt unhappy because she had not yet found the love of her life. One day, while walking in the palace garden, she heard the singing of a beautiful bird with bright blue feathers. No one had ever seen a bird like this before.

Princess Leila thought that the Blue Bird might be the key to her happiness, so she decided to search for it. She asked her father, the king, to announce a contest in which all the participants must search for the Blue Bird and bring it to her. The king agreed to the idea and announced the contest to all the young men in the kingdom.

Many young men came to the palace to participate in the contest and search for the Blue Bird. Among them was a poor young man named Yassin. Yassin was in love with Princess Leila and wanted to make her happy by finding the Blue Bird. He did not have wealth or a position that would be suitable for the princess, but he had intelligence, bravery, and determination.

Yassin began his long journey to search for the Blue Bird. Days, weeks, and months passed without any success. On this journey, he faced many challenges and dangers, but he did not give up. During his journey, Yassin met many people who helped him and provided him with new information about the whereabouts of the Blue Bird.

In the end, Yassin discovered that the Blue Bird lived on a remote island in the middle of the sea. He decided to sail to this island to find the bird and bring it back to Princess Leila. After many days of suffering and violent storms at sea, Yassin arrived at the remote island.

Yassin explored the island and faced many obstacles and strange creatures, but he did not give up. After a long search and perseverance, Yassin found the Blue Bird and managed to catch it. With great joy, Yassin returned to the kingdom with the Blue Bird.

When Yassin returned and showed the Blue Bird to Princess Leila, everyone's hearts filled with happiness and amazement. The king celebrated Yassin's return and announced his victory in the contest. But Princess Leila did not only want the Blue Bird; she also wanted the young man who went to the ends of the earth to make her happy.

Princess Leila married Yassin with the approval of the king and queen. Yassin and Princess Leila lived a happy life filled with love and prosperity. The story taught King Shahryar and the people that determination, bravery, and love could overcome any challenge and lead to true happiness.

And so, the eighth chapter of the Tales of One Thousand and One Nights came to an end. King Shahryar could only wait eagerly for the next night to hear another inspiring and exciting story from Scheherazade.

On the following night, King Shahryar and Scheherazade gathered again, where the king was eager to hear more inspiring and exciting stories. King Shahryar felt that these stories had changed his life for the better and taught him valuable lessons about justice, wisdom, and love.

And so, Scheherazade continued to tell her stories to King Shahryar night after night, trying to teach him and his people more important lessons about life and humanity.

Questions
1. What was Princess Leila feeling and why?
2. What did Princess Leila ask her father, the king, for?
3. Who is Yasin, and what made him participate in the competition?
4. Where did Yasin learn that the blue bird lived?
5. What happened when Yasin returned with the blue bird to the kingdom?

6. How did people's lives improve in the kingdom after the princess's return?

Answers

1. Princess Leila was feeling sad because she had not found the love of her life.
2. Princess Leila asked her father, the king, to announce a competition to search for and bring her the blue bird.
3. Yasin is a poor young man who is in love with Princess Leila and wants to make her happy by bringing her the blue bird.
4. Yasin learned that the blue bird lived on a remote island in the middle of the sea.
5. Everyone's hearts were filled with joy and amazement when Yasin returned with the blue bird. The king celebrated his victory in the competition, and Princess Leila married Yasin.

الفصل التّاسِع
البِنْت و السّاحِرة

في اللّيْلة اللي بعْدها، اِسْتعدّ الملِك شهْرَيار علشان يِسْمع حِكايَة جِديدة مِن شهْرزاد. بدأِت شهْرزاد تِحْكي حِكايةْ البِنْت و السّاحِرة.

في يوْم مِن الأيّامْ، في قرْيَة بِعيدة، كان فيه بِنْت شابّة إسْمها لينا. كانِت لينا ساكْنة معَ مامِتْها العيّانة و أخوها الصُّغيّر. كانوا فُقرا و

بِيْكافْحوا علشان يادوْب يِوَفّروا اِحْتِياجاتْهُم اليَوْمية. في يوْم مِن الأيّام، راحِت لينا الغابة علشان تِجمّع عيْش الغُراب و التّوت لِأُسْرِتْها. و هِيَّ بِتِتْمشّى في الغابة، سِمْعِت صوْت ضعيف بِيْنادى عليْها.

مِشْيِت لينا وَرا الصّوْت لِغايِةْ ما لِقِت سِتّ عجوزة. كانِت السِّتّ هزيلة و ضعيفة، و كانِت بِتْحاوِل تِحْمي نفْسها مِن البرْد. لمّا لينا شافت حالِتْها الصّعْبة، قرّرِت تِساعِدْها. فا خدِت السِّتّ لِبيْتْها و قدِّمْتِلها أكْل و مكان تِنام فيه. على الرّغْم مِن الفقْر اللي كانِت أُسْرِتْها عايْشة فيه، لكِن لينا كانِت كريمة و حنونة.

بعْد ما السِّتّ اِسْتعادِت قُوّتْها، قالِت لِلينا إنّها في الحقيقة ساحِرة قَوية. و على سبيل الاِمْتِنان لِلينا علشان طيبِةْ قلْبها و كرمْها، عرضِت السّاحِرة على لينا تِحقّقْلها تلات أُمْنِيّات. فكّرِت لينا شُوَيّة و قرّرِت تُطْلُب الشّفا لِمامِتْها، و تحْسين حَياةْ أخوها، و الثّرْوَة علشان تِوَفّر حَياة أحْسن لِأُسْرِتْها.

وافْقِت السّاحِرة على تحْقيق أُمْنيّات لينا، و حسّنِت حَياةْ أُسْرتْها. رِجِعِت الصِّحّة و النّشاط لِمامةْ لينا، و أخوها قِدِر يروح المدْرسة و يِتعلِّم. و بِفضْل الثّرْوَة اللي جتْلُهُم، قِدْرِت عيْلةْ لينا تِبْني بيْت جِديد و تِوَفَّر حَياة مُريحة لأفْرادْها.

مرِّت السِّنين، و اِتْحسِّنِت أحْوال الأُسْرة بِفضْل المُساعْدة السِّحْرية. كِبْرِت لينا و بقِت بِنْت حِلْوَة و ذكِية و شُجاعة. كانِت دايماً فاكْرة عطْف السّاحِرة عليْها و على أُسْرتْها، و عشان كِده قرّرِت تِساعِد النّاس في قِرْيتْها. بقِت معْروفة بِحِكْمِتْها و رحْمِتْها، عشان كانِت بِتْقدِّم المشورة و المُساعْدة لِجيرانْها.

في يوْمْ مِن الأيّام، قرّب مِن لينا شابّ غِريب و طلب مُساعْدِتْها. كانِت القرْيَة مُهدّدة مِن مجْموعةْ حرامية عايْزين يِسْرقوا أمْلاك النّاس و يِرعِّبوهُم. اِسْتعانِت لينا بِذكاءْها و شجاعِتْها علشان تِنظّم الفلّاحين و تِقاوِم اللُّصوص. بعْد المُواجْهة الشّرِسة، قِدْروا يِهْزِموا اللُّصوص و يِحْموا القرْيَة.

بِفضْل شجاعتْها و حِكْمِتْها، بقِت لينا قائِدة ليها اِحْترامْها في قرْيِتْها. اِتْجوِّزِت الشابّ اللي طلب مُساعْدِتْها، و عملوا عيْلة جديدة معَ بعْض. عاشِت لينا حَياة سعيدة و مُسْتقِّرة، و فِضْلِت تِساعِد القرْيَة بحِكْمِتْها و قُوِّتْها. كِسْبِت حُبّ و اِحْترام كُلّ النّاس اللي في القرْيَة علشان كُلّ التّضْحِيّات و المُساعْدات اللي قدِّمِتْها.

خلّصِت شهْرزاد قِصّة البِنْت و السّاحِرة العجوزة، و كان الملِك شهْريَار بيِسْمع القِصّة و هُوَّ مُتشوِّق. و رغْم إنّها كانِت قِصّة مُخْتلِفة عن القِصص اللي قبْلها، بسّ هُوَّ اِسْتمْتع بيها و كان مُتحمِّس لِسماع القِصّة اللي بعْدها.

Questions

1. أيه اللي كانِت لينا بِتِعْمِلُه في الغابة قبْل ما تْقابِل السِّتّ العجوزة؟

2. إزّاي لينا ساعْدِت السِّتّ العجوزة؟

3. أيه الحاجة اللي السِّتّ العجوزة كشفِتْها عن نفْسها بعْد ما اسْتعادِت قُوِّتْها؟

4. أيه التّلات أُمْنِيّات اللي طلبِتْهُم لينا مِن السّاحِرة؟

5. إزّاي لينا أنْقذِت قرْيِتْها مِن مجْموعِةْ الحرامية؟

Answers

1. كانِت لينا بِتْجمّع عيْش الغُراب و التّوت في الغابة علشان أُسرتِها.

2. أخدِت لينا السِّتّ العجوزة لِبيْتها و قدِّمِتْلها أكْل و مكان تِنام فيه.

3. كشفِت السِّتّ العجوزة إنّها في الحقيقة ساحِرة قَوية.

4. إنّ أمّها تِخِفّ، و تحْسين حَياةْ أخوها، و الثّرْوَة عشان تِوَفّر حَياة أحْسن لأُسْرتِها.

5. اِسْتعانِت لينا بِذكاءْها و شجاعتْها علشان تِنظّم الفلّاحين و تِتْواجِهْ اللُّصوص. و بعْد المُواجْهة الشرِسة، قِدْروا يِهْزِموا اللُّصوص و يِحْموا القرْيَة.

Chapter 9: The Girl and the Magical Old Woman

On the next night, King Shahryar prepared himself to listen to a new story from Scheherazade. Scheherazade began to narrate the story of the girl and the sorceress.

Once upon a time, in a faraway village, there was a young girl named Lena. Lena lived with her sick mother and younger brother. They were poor and struggled to make ends meet. One day, Lena went to the forest to gather mushrooms and berries for her family. While wandering in the forest, she heard a weak voice calling her.

Lena followed the voice until she reached an old woman. The old woman appeared frail and weak, and she was trying to shelter from the cold. When Lena saw her miserable condition, she decided to help her. The girl took the old woman to her house, where she provided her with food and shelter. Despite the poverty that her family lived in, Lena was kind and compassionate.

After the old woman regained her strength, she revealed to Lena that she was actually a powerful sorceress. In gratitude for Lena's kindness and generosity, the sorceress offered Lena three wishes. Lena thought about it and decided to ask for her mother's healing, to improve her brother's life, and wealth to provide a better life for her family.

The sorceress agreed to fulfill Lena's wishes and transformed the family's life for the better. Lena's mother became healthy and active again, and her brother was able to go to school and learn. Thanks to the wealth they acquired, Lena's family was able to build a new house and provide a comfortable life for themselves.

Years passed, and the family flourished thanks to the magical help. Lena grew up to become a beautiful, intelligent, and brave girl. She always remembered the sorceress's kindness to her and her family and therefore decided to help others in her village. She became known for her wisdom and compassion, offering advice and assistance to her neighbors.

One day, a strange young man approached Lena and asked for her help. The village was threatened by a group of thieves who sought to steal people's possessions and intimidate them. Lena used her intelligence and courage to organize the villagers and confront the thieves. After a fierce confrontation, they managed to defeat the thieves and secure the village.

Thanks to her courage and wisdom, Lena became a respected leader in her village. She married the young man who asked for her help, and they started a new family together. Lena lived a happy and stable life and continued to help the village with her wisdom and strength. She won the love and respect of all the villagers for her sacrifices and assistance.

Scheherazade finished narrating the story of the girl and the sorceress, and King Shahryar eagerly listened to the story. Although it was a different story from the previous ones, he enjoyed it and was eager to hear the next story.

Questions

1. What was Lena doing in the forest before meeting the old woman?
2. How did Lena help the old woman?
3. What did the old woman reveal about herself after regaining her strength?
4. What were the three wishes that Lena asked the sorceress for?
5. How did Lena rescue her village from the group of thieves?

Answers

1. Lena was collecting mushrooms and berries for her family in the forest.
2. Lena took he old woman to her home and provided her with food and shelter.
3. The old woman revealed that she was actually a powerful sorceress.

4. To heal her mother, improve her brother's life, and gain wealth to provide a better life for her family.

5. Lena relied on her intelligence and bravery to organize the villagers and confront the thieves, and after a fierce confrontation, they were able to defeat the thieves and secure the village.

الفَصْل العاشِر
الأمير و التِّنين

في اللّيْلة اللي بعْدها، بدأِت شهْرزاد تِحْكي حِكايةْ الأمير و التِّنين لِلْملِك شهْرَيار.

في ممْلكة بِعيدة، كان فيه أمير شابّ و شُجاع إسْمُه رامي. المملْكة كانِت بِتْعاني مِن هجمات مُتكرِّرة مِن تِنين عِمْلاق عايش في جبل

قُرَيِّب. التِّنِّين كان بِيْهاجِم القُرى و بِيْخْطف الشَّباب و البنات عشان ياكُلْهُم. النَّاس كانوا عايْشين في خوْف طول الوَقْت و مكانوش بِيْجْرُؤوا يِواجْهوا التِّنِّين العِمْلاق.

في يوْم مِن الأيّام، قابِل الأمير رامي راجِل مِن قرْيَة مِن القُرى المنْكوبة. قالُه الرّاجِل: "يا أميرْنا، التِّنِّين خطف بِنْتي الصُّغيّرة، و بقيْنا عايْشين في خوْف مِش قادْرين نِتْحمِّلُه. أرْجوك تِنْقِذْنا مِن الوَحْش المُرْعِب ده."

قرَّر الأمير رامي إنُّه يِواجِه التِّنِّين و يِنْقِذ شعْبُه مِن الكائِن المُرْعِب ده. سلّح نفسُه بأحْسن الأسْلِحة و الدُّروع و اِبْتدى رِحْلِتُه لِجبل التِّنِّين. و أثناء رِحْلِتُه، قابِل حكيم عُجوز إدّالُه سِلاح سِحْري يقدر يِهْزم التِّنِّين بيه. قالُه الحكيم: "اِسْتخْدِم السِّلاح السِّحْري ده بِحذر، ده الشّيْء الوَحيد اللي مُمْكِن يِهْزِم التِّنِّين العِمْلاق."

وِصِل الأمير رامى لِجبل التِّنِّين و لِقي الوَحْش الكبير نايِم. قرّر يِسْتنّى لِحدّ ما التِّنِّين يِصْحى عشان

يِواجهُه بِشجاعة. لمَّا صِحي التِّنين، زعق الأمير رامى و قالُّه: "يا تِنين يا شِرِّير، أنا هقْضي عليْك النَّهارْده و هنْقِذ شعْبي مِن هجماتك الوَحْشية!"

اِستعدَّ لِمُواجْهةِ التِّنين، و اِسْتخْدِم السِّلاح السِّحْري اللي الحكيم العجوز إدَّاهولُه. بدأت المعْركة بين الأمير رامى و التِّنين العِمْلاق. كان التِّنين بيرفْرف بِجناحاتُه و بيْطلَّع النَّار مِن بُقُّه في اِتِّجاه الأمير، و في نفْس الوَقْت كان رامى بيتْجنَّبُه بِمهارة و بيسْتخْدِم سِلاحُه السِّحْري عشان يِوَجِّهْ لِلتِّنين ضربات قَوية. اِستمرَّت المعْركة لِساعات طَويلة، و كان الأمير رامى بيِفْقِد قُوُّتُه شُوَيَّة بِشْوَيَّة.

في لحْظة حاسِمة، اِسْتعان رامى بِكلّ شجاعتُه و بِالْقُوة اللي فِضْلِت عنْدُه، و قِدِر يِوَجِّهْ ضرْبة قاضْية لِلتِّنين بِسِلاحُه السِّحْري. وقع التِّنين على الأرْض و مات، و بِكِده أنْقذ الأمير رامى شعْبُه مِن الوَحْش المُرْعِب.

رِجِع الأمير رامى لِلْمملكة، و كان النَّاس مِسْتنْيِّينُه عشان يِحْتِفْلوا

بِبُطولْتُه. اِتْجمّعوا في ساحات المدينة و عملوا مهرجان كبير عشان يِحْتِفْلوا بِالأمير الشُّجاع. اِتْجوِّز رامى أجْمل بِنْت في المملكة و ورِث العرْش لمّا مات أبوهُ الملِك.

حكم رامى المملكة بِحِكْمة و عدْل، و بقى معْروف بِشجاعْتُه و تضْحِيّاتُه عشان شعْبُه. عاشِت المملكة في سلام و رخاء تحْتَ حُكْمُه العادِل و اِنْتهِت مُعاناتْهُم مِن هجمات التِّنين أوّ أيّ خطر تاني. و دي كانِت حِكايةِ الأمير رامى و التِّنين العِمْلاق اللي حكِتْها شهْرزاد للْملِك شهْرَيار.

بعْد ما سِمِع الملِك شهْرَيار حِكايةِ الأمير رامي و التِّنين، أبْدى إعْجاب شِديد بِشجاعةِ الأمير و حِكْمِتُه في حُكْم المملكة. و كان بِيسْألْ نفْسُه، يا ترى، أيْه هَيِحْصل لوْ قِدِر يِتْعلّم مِن تجارِب الأمير رامي و يِطبّقْها في ممْلكْتُه. فكّر الملِك بِعُمْق في القِصص اللي سِمِعْها مِن شهْرزاد، و اِبْتدى يِشوف نفْسُه بِمنْظور جِديد.

قرّر الملِك شهْرَيار إنّه مَيقْتِلْش شهْرزاد، مِش بسّ عشان كان عايِز يِسْمع حِكاياتْها كُلّ ليْلة، بسّ كمان عشان الحِكايات بتاعِتْها كان ليها تأْثير كِبير على شخْصِيّتُه و غيّرِتُه للْأحْسن. بقى ملِك عادِل أكْتر، و ألْطف، بِفضْل الحِكايات دي اللي ألْهِمتُه و علّمِتُه قيمةْ الرّحْمة و الإنْصاف.

في الأيّام اللي بعْدها، أصْبح الملِك شهْرَيار أكْتر عدْل و رحْمة في حُكْمُه. بقى يِسْمع باهْتِمام لِشكاوي شعْبُه، و انْشغل بِتصْحيح الظُّلْم و تحْسين حَياةْ النّاس. اتْحوَّلِت المملكة لِمكان أحْسن لِلْحَياة تحْتَ حُكْم الملِك شهْرَيار العادِل.

عاش الملِك شهْرَيار و شهْرزاد سَوا في سعادة و رخاء لِسنين طَويلة. و فِضْلِت شهْرزاد تِحْكي الحِكايات لِجوْزْها الملِك شهْرَيار كُلّ ليْلة، و كانِت الحِكايات دي سِرّ سعادِتْهُم و سعادةْ ممْلكِتْهُم. و بِكِده انْتِهت حِكايةْ شهْرزاد و الملِك شهْرَيار اللي غيّرِت مصير ممْلكة بِحالْها.

Questions

1. أيْه اللي كانِت المَمْلكة بِتْعاني مِنُّه بِسبب التِّنين العِمْلاق؟

2. أيْه اللي قرّر الأمير رامي يعْمِلُه لمّا سِمِع عن مُعاناةْ النّاس من التِّنين؟

3. الأمير رامى جاب السِّلاح السِّحْري مِنيْن؟

4. إزّاي الأمير رامى قِدِر يِهْزِم التِّنين؟

5. إزّاي النّاس اِحْتفلوا بعْد هزيمةْ التِّنين؟

6. أيْه اللي سألُه المَلِك شهْرَيار لِنفْسُه بعْد ما سِمِع قِصَّةْ الأمير رامى و التِّنين؟

7. إزّاي اِتْأثَّر المَلِك شهْرَيار بِقِصص شهْرزاد؟

8. إزّاي إتغيرت المَمْلكة تحْتَ حُكْم المَلِك شهْرَيار؟

9. إزّاي أثَّرِت قِصص شهْرزاد على حَياةْ المَلِك شهْرَيار و شهْرزاد معَ بعْض؟

10. إِزَّاي اِنْتِهِت حِكايةْ شهْرزاد و الملِك شهْرَيار؟

Answers

1. كانِت المملْكة بِتْعاني مِن هجمات مُتكرِّرة لِلتِّنين العِمْلاق اللي كان بِيْهاجِم القُرى و يِخطف الشْباب و البنات عشان ياكُلْهُم.

2. قرّر الأمير رامي يِواجِهْ التِّنين و يِنْقِذ شعْبُه مِن الوَحْش المُرْعِب ده.

3. الأمير رامى جاب السِّلاح السِّحْري مِن حكيم عجوز قابلُه في رِحْلِتُه لِجبل التِّنين.

4. قِدِر الأمير رامى يِهْزِم التِّنين بِاسْتِخْدام السِّلاح السِّحْري اللي إدّاهولُه الحكيم العجوز، و وَجِّهْ بيه ضرْبة قاضْيَة لِلتِّنين.

5. النّاس اِحْتفلوا بعْد هزيمِةْ التِّنين بِإنُّهُم اِتْجمّعوا في ساحات المدينة و عملوا مهْرجان كِبير عشان يِحْتِفْلوا بِالأمير الشُّجاع رامى.

6. المَلِك شهْرَيار سأل نفسُه يا ترى، أيْه اللي هَيِحْصل لَوْ قِدِر يِتْعلِّم مِن تجارُب الأمير رامي و يطبَّقْها في ممْلكْتُه.

7. اِتْأثَّر المَلِك شهْرَيار بِشكْل عميق بِقِصص شهْرزاد اللي ألْهِمِتُه و علَّمِتُه قيمِةْ الرَّحْمة و الإنْصاف، و بقى ملِك أكْتر عادِل أكْتر، و ألْطف.

8. اِتحوَّلِت ممْلكة لِمكان أفْضل لِلْحَياة تحْتَ حُكْم المَلِك شهْرَيار العادِل، لِإنُّه بقى بِيِسْمع بِاِهْتِمام لِشكاوي شعْبُه و اِنْشغل بِتِصْحيح الظُّلْم و تحْسين حَياةْ النّاس.

9. عاش المَلِك شهْرَيار و شهْرزاد معَ بعْض في سعادة و اِزْدِهار لِسِنين طَويلة، و فِضْلِت شهْرزاد تِحْكي الحِكايات لِجوْزْها المَلِك شهْرَيار كُلّ لَيْلة، و كانِت القِصص دي سِرّ سعادِتْهُم و سعادة ممْلكِتْهُم.

10. اِنْتهِت حِكايةْ شهْرزاد و المَلِك شهْرَيار بِتغْيير مصير ممْلكة بِحالْها، و عاشوا معَ بعْض في سعادة و اِزْدِهار لِسِنين طَويلة،

فِضْلِت شهْرزاد تِحْكي القِصص لِجوزْها الملِك شهْرَيار كُلّ ليْلة، و ساهْمِت القِصص دي في تحْسين علاقِتْهُم و عمل تغْييرات إيجابية على مُسْتَوى المملْكة بِحالْها.

Chapter 10: The Prince and the Dragon

On the next night, Scheherazade began to tell the story of the prince and the dragon to King Shahryar.

In a faraway kingdom, there was a young and brave prince named Rami. The kingdom suffered from frequent attacks by a huge dragon that lived in a nearby mountain. The dragon would attack the villages and kidnap young boys and girls to eat them. The people lived in constant fear and did not dare to confront the giant dragon.

One day, Prince Rami met a man from one of the devastated villages. The man said to him, "Oh, our prince, the dragon has kidnapped my little daughter, and we live in unbearable fear. I beg you to save us from this terrifying monster."

Prince Rami decided to face the dragon and save his people from this terrifying creature. He prepared himself with the best weapons and armor and set out on his journey to the dragon's mountain. During his journey, he met a wise old man who gave him a magic weapon that could defeat the dragon. The wise man said to the prince, "Use this magic weapon carefully, for it is the only one that can defeat the giant dragon."

Prince Rami reached the dragon's mountain and found the huge monster sleeping. He decided to wait until the dragon woke up to face him bravely. When the dragon woke up,

Prince Rami shouted, "Oh, evil dragon, today I will kill you and save my people from your brutal attacks!"

He prepared to face the dragon and used the magic weapon given to him by the wise old man. The battle began between Prince Rami and the huge dragon. The dragon flapped its wings and breathed fire at the prince while Rami dodged skillfully and used his magic weapon to strike hard blows at the dragon. The battle continued for hours, and Prince Rami was slowly losing his energy.

In a decisive moment, Rami summoned all his courage and remaining strength and managed to deliver a fatal blow to the dragon using his magic weapon. The dragon fell to the ground and breathed its last breath, and thus, Prince Rami saved his people from the terrifying monster.

Prince Rami returned to the kingdom, where people awaited him eagerly to celebrate his bravery. They gathered in the city squares and held a big festival in honor of the brave prince. Rami married one of the most beautiful girls in the kingdom and inherited the throne when his father, the king, died.

Prince Rami ruled the kingdom wisely and fairly and became known for his courage and sacrifices for his people. The kingdom lived in peace and prosperity under his fair rule and did not suffer any more dragon attacks or other risks. This was the story of Prince Rami and the huge dragon told by Scheherazade to King Shahryar.

After hearing the story of Prince Rami and the dragon, King Shahryar expressed his deep admiration for the prince's bravery and wisdom in ruling his kingdom. He wondered what it would be like if he could learn from Prince Rami's experiences and apply them to his own kingdom. King Shahryar reflected on the stories he had heard from Scheherazade and began to see himself in a new light.

King Shahryar decided not to kill Scheherazade not only because he looked forward to hearing her stories every night, but also because her stories had a profound effect on his personality and had changed him for the better. He became a more just and kind king thanks to those stories that inspired him and taught him the value of mercy and fairness.

In the following days, King Shahryar became more just and merciful in his rule. He listened carefully to his people's complaints and worked hard to correct the injustice and improve people's lives. The kingdom turned into a better place to live under King Shahryar's fair rule.

King Shahryar and Scheherazade lived together in happiness and prosperity for many years. Scheherazade continued to tell stories to her husband, King Shahryar, every night, and those stories were the secret to their happiness and the happiness of their kingdom. And thus ended the story of Scheherazade and King Shahryar, which changed the fate of the entire kingdom.

Questions

1. What was the kingdom suffering from because of the giant dragon?
2. What did Prince Rami decide when he heard about the people's suffering from the dragon?
3. Where did Prince Rami get the magical weapon from?
4. How did Prince Rami manage to defeat the dragon?
5. How did the people celebrate after defeating the dragon?
6. What did King Shahryar wonder about after hearing the story of Prince Rami and the dragon?
7. How was King Shahryar affected by the stories of Scheherazade?
8. How did the kingdom change under King Shahryar's rule?
9. How did the stories of Scheherazade affect the lives of King Shahryar and Scheherazade together?
10. How did the story of Scheherazade and King Shahryar end?

Answers

1. The kingdom was suffering from frequent attacks by the giant dragon that would attack villages and kidnap young boys and girls to eat them.

2. Prince Rami decided to confront the dragon and save his people from this terrifying monster.

3. Prince Rami obtained the magical weapon from a wise old man he met during his journey to the dragon mountain.

4. Prince Rami managed to defeat the dragon by using the magical weapon given to him by the wise old man and delivering a fatal blow to the dragon.

5. The people celebrated after defeating the dragon by gathering in the city squares and holding a big festival to honor the brave Prince Rami.

6. King Shahryar wondered how it would be if he could learn from Prince Rami's experiences and apply them in his own kingdom.

7. King Shahryar was deeply influenced by the stories of Scheherazade, which inspired him and taught him the value of mercy and justice, and he became a more just and kind king.

8. The kingdom became a better place to live under the rule of the just King Shahryar, who listened carefully

to the complaints of his people and worked hard to correct injustices and improve their lives.

9. King Shahryar and Scheherazade lived together in happiness and prosperity for many years, with Scheherazade continuing to tell stories to her husband every night, and those stories were the secret of their happiness and the happiness of their kingdom.

10. The story of Scheherazade and King Shahryar ended with the change of the fate of the entire kingdom and making them live together in happiness and prosperity for many years, with Scheherazade continuing to tell stories to her husband every night, and these stories helped to strengthen their bond and bring about positive changes throughout the kingdom.

lingualism

Visit our website for information on current and upcoming titles and free language learning resources.

www.lingualism.com

www.ingramcontent.com/pod-product-compliance
Lightning Source LLC
Chambersburg PA
CBHW062034120526
44592CB00036B/2096